T0197199

Get Out of Your Head and into Your Heart Integrating the Mind and Heart

An Intuitive Perspective in Transformation

SUZI USDANE WALL, MSW, LCSW

BALBOA.PRESS

A DIVISION OF HAY HOUSE

Balboa Press books may be ordered through booksellers or by contacting:

Balboa Press
A Division of Hay House
1663 Liberty Drive
Bloomington, IN 47403
www.balboapress.com
844-682-1282

Because of the dynamic nature of the Internet, any web addresses or links contained in this book may have changed since publication and may no longer be valid. The views expressed in this work are solely those of the author and do not necessarily reflect the views of the publisher, and the publisher hereby disclaims any responsibility for them.

The author of this book does not dispense medical advice or prescribe the use of any technique as a form of treatment for physical, emotional, or medical problems without the advice of a physician, either directly or indirectly. The intent of the author is only to offer information of a general nature to help you in your quest for emotional and spiritual well-being. In the event you use any of the information in this book for yourself, which is your constitutional right, the author and the publisher assume no responsibility for your actions.

The Author and Publisher have made every effort to ensure the information in this book was correct at Press Time. The Author and Publisher do not assume and hereby disclaim any liability to any party for any loss, damage, disruption caused by errors, omissions, or any other inconsistencies herein. This publication is meant as a source of valuable information for the reader, however it is not meant as a substitute for direct expert assistance. If such a level of assistance is required, the services of a competent professional should be sought

Any people depicted in stock imagery provided by Getty Images are models, and such images are being used for illustrative purposes only. Certain stock imagery © Getty Images.

Print information available on the last page.

ISBN: 979-8-7652-3781-6 (sc)
ISBN: 979-8-7652-3783-0 (hc)
ISBN: 979-8-7652-3782-3 (e)

Library of Congress Control Number: 2023902292

Balboa Press rev. date: 04/28/2023

CONTENTS

INTRODUCTION

It All Begins Here

Find a balance between head and heart.

—Colleen Hoover

I created this book out of a desire to make a difference in people's lives. It is my hope that anyone reading this book will take time to process it, reflect on the details, and learn new tools and strategies to assist in making their life paths their own. I also hope that, in time, the reader will understand this title and begin the process of listening to his or her heart. Therefore, this journey begins. It focuses on what I call the five plus one, which includes our senses of feeling, seeing, hearing, tasting, touching, and knowing.

In 2015, a few of my clients began talking to me about writing a book that taught some of the tools they learned during their counseling sessions. They said, "If you write a book and teach these tools, you will be helping so many people." One person laughed and said, "Suzi, it would be more helpful if you wrote a book with all these tools. This would make our lives easier, and we would not have to write down so many notes in session. Also, maybe it could be helpful for other people." After learning these tools, they often reported gaining additional insight and awareness in identifying feelings and other techniques which helped in their daily lives. Therefore, my goal of creating this book became a reality. I want to express appreciation and gratitude to these people who not only made a difference in my life but, I hope, in yours as well.

I want to thank my wonderful family, my husband, and my two adult children, who light up my days and bring joy and blessing to my life. I want to thank my extended family for being in my life and supporting me along my way and of course, my father in heaven, who guides me daily. To my friends, I say thank you for helping me laugh and smile and for bringing me happiness.

In addition, I want to honor three people whose teachings have provided benefit to my life.

Louise Hay and her book *You Can Heal Your Life* inspired me to start my own journey of self-reflection when I was an adolescent. Dr. Wayne Dyer, a psychologist, assisted me in my educational growth. His story and books encouraged me to focus on helping others to help themselves. The third person is Lisa Williams, who brought me passion and joy from the first time I saw her. I felt uplifted as I sat on the couch with my seven-year-old son when he practiced for his part as the narrator in the musical *Joseph and the Amazing Technicolor Dreamcoat*. That day, he emulated Lisa and her talent. Years later, I sat in a conference at Celebrate Your Life and realized this was the same Lisa I saw so many years ago. She was one of the headlining speakers making a difference in my life once more. I believe very strongly that the past, present, and future are interconnected, and if we are focused on the present, all will align. This is where the past, present, and future connect in my life.

I was a sophomore at the University of Arizona and was excited to audition to become an aerobics instructor. I was dressed in my black leotard and favorite pink satin embroidered jacket. I got into my car and began to drive back to my apartment to share the news of becoming an aerobics instructor with my roommates. However, I never arrived home.

I was driving down Speedway Boulevard towards my apartment in Tucson when suddenly I saw a car driving out of control. I remember my body tightening as I saw the car getting closer. Then I heard the shattering of the metal, saw the flashes of the sparks, and felt the spinning of the car. It did not stop there. I saw the car approaching again. This time, the car hit me head-on, and then spun to the other side of the street before hitting a pole. I was coming in and out of consciousness as I heard the sirens approaching. I prayed, "Please help me."

I remember hearing outside the car window the emergency medical technicians talking about how to remove me from the car. Coming in and out of consciousness, I heard them talk about removing me with the jaws of life. I felt trapped, frightened, and confused, and then everything went dark.

This was the first of four car accidents I have experienced in my life. That accident filled me with pain and fear of the unknown. Through my years of healing, education, and growth, I have learned and implemented tools and strategies that I hope to teach you throughout this book. These tools are great resources to use and implement in your lives, and I look forward to collaborating with you on your own journey of getting out of your head and into your heart.

This book will include education, stories, thought-provoking ideas, and exercises to complete. Take your time reading this book. Skip ahead, go back, and just be present in each moment as you read, learn, and grow.

Please be aware that all names and stories have been modified or changed unless an individual granted permission. If an individual has shared personal information, I honor and thank that person for being kind, supportive, vulnerable, and allowing others to learn and grow through his or her life experiences.

Welcome aboard.

CHAPTER 1

Start at the Beginning: Mind and Heart

It is confidence in our bodies, minds, and spirits that

allows us to keep looking for new adventures.

—Oprah Winfrey

The title of this book may be scary for you. Whether you realize it or not, we live in our heads. We focus on the constant thoughts that may not always be real. This title challenges you to get out of your head and into your heart. One of the ways we do that is through integration. The word *integration* brings up ideas such as blending, merging, and weaving concepts together. It is important to define the words in the title to assist you in understanding their meanings and their importance, both from an intellectual and a spiritual perspective. In addition, the many quotations and stories in this book will assist in enhancing words, meanings, and the learning process. It is my belief that integration has the ability to bring about change in many areas of life. Let us begin with the definitions of meaningful words in the title. The first word to understand is *integration*.

Integration comes from the Latin word meaning whole. It is the act or instance of combining things into an integral whole.[1] The word *integration*, often spoken about in the medical and mental health fields indicates striving to bring two concepts together and then sharing the benefits with one another.

Think about the medical community, filled with many medical practitioners. Some of these are MDs (medical doctors), NPs (naturopathic doctors), DOs (doctors of osteopathic medicine), PAs (physician's assistants), and NPs (nurse practitioners). These medical practitioners have specializations in many medical areas. Training for these professions is both similar and different. These professionals give patients options and the possibility of implementing more than one type of medical care. Many of these medical practitioners integrate the traditional medical approach with an alternative medical approach. This assists patients in their health care and well-being, which brings us back to the primary word: *integration*.

---

[1] *Merriam-Webster*, s.v. "integration (*n.*)," accessed October 27, 2022, https://www.merriam-webster.com/dictionary/integration.

The Story of Integration

> Wholeness is not achieved by cutting off a portion of
> one's being, but by integration of the contraries.
>
> —Carl Jung

In my life, I have unfortunately experienced four car accidents, all caused by other drivers. Because of these car accidents, I have many injuries and at times suffer with pain. In addition, I have worked with many doctors, physical therapists, massage therapists, psychologists, and other medical practitioners. They assisted me with my work on healing physically, psychologically, and spiritually. I integrated these specialty areas, working with practitioners to create better healing for my mind and body.

The first of these car accidents occurred in 1982 and the most recent was in 1996. I struggled to work and was unable to use my right arm or hand initially. I was attending the University of Arizona, and at one point, university personnel spoke to me about taking time off to heal and then return to school. For me, that was unacceptable. Instead, I set off to devise a plan to make college work in my life with my pain, injuries, doctors, and limitations.

The university allowed me to work with student helpers who assisted with note taking because I was not able to use my right arm or hand. However, I began learning to use my left hand to write. Initially, my writing was very messy, but with much practice, work, and commitment, my plan allowed me to complete the semester at the university, pain and all.

At the time, my injuries were extensive. I wore a neck brace for two years, worked with many different types of doctors, and received trigger injections and nerve blocks in my head and neck every few weeks. I was on medications that often did not help and made me physically ill. At times, I was fearful of getting in the car, driving, and having it happen again.

I met with over thirty doctors that my father helped me find, received all types of treatments, and created a plan that I believed could help. I felt strongly that if I believed and worked on strengthening my muscles around the injured areas, I would start to heal my body.

I worked very hard researching and participating in medical treatments. I was constantly researching to find techniques to help me with the pain. I taught myself and implemented diaphragmatic breathing, visualization, and quieting my thoughts.

As defined in *Medical News Today*,

> Diaphragmatic breathing, or "belly breathing," involves fully engaging the stomach, abdominal muscles, and diaphragm, when breathing. This means actively

pulling the diaphragm down with each inward breath. In this way, diaphragmatic breathing helps the lungs fill more efficiently.[2]

In my treatment, every two weeks I met with my doctor, a kind and supportive anesthesiologist who worked at Good Samaritan Hospital in Phoenix, Arizona. The treatment included trigger injections and nerve blocks in my head, neck, and back. The first time he completed this treatment, the pain was so intense that I actually passed out. I decided there must be some technique to move away from the pain and not pass out every two weeks. I began researching to teach myself techniques of breathing, visualization, and ways to move away from my pain. This will be discussed later in the book.

The Mind

Put your heart, mind, and soul into even your

smallest acts. This is the secret of success.

—Swami Sivananda

The second word in the title is *mind*. When I think about the definition of the mind, words such as thinking, reasoning, remembering

---

[2] Jon Johnson, "What to know about diaphragmatic breathing," Medical News Today, posted May 27, 2020, https://www.medicalnewstoday.com/articles/diaphragmatic-breathing#summary.

are brought forward. This unique organ allows individuals to become aware of the world and their experiences, to think in a concrete or abstract manner, and to analyze the thoughts.

Our minds and brains are intricate organs that assist us in ways that are both positive and negative. We can have positive or negative thinking, positive or negative self-talk, and a positive or negative self-image. The positive can create motivation and success, and the negative can create worry, racing thoughts, and, at times, anxiety. When we focus on the positive, we become aware of how to use our minds in a healthy way and enhance our lives.

The Heart

> The best and most beautiful things in the world cannot
> be seen or touched—they must be felt with the heart.
> —Helen Keller

The third word in the title is *heart*. When we focus on the word *heart*, we feel our emotions and reactions. In the *American Heritage Dictionary*, one definition of the word *heart* is the repository of one's deepest emotions, feelings, and beliefs[3]. The heart is a very important organ, both physically and emotionally. We cannot live without

---

[3] *The American Heritage Dictionary of the English Language*, 4th ed. (2000), s.v. "heart."

it. In fact, we know that physically, the heart is imperative to our lives. However, often it does not get the credit it deserves. It assists in determining our genuineness, the emotions that we feel, and the state of our well-being. At times, people are fearful of their emotions and may withdraw or shut down feelings. We will explore this later in the book.

Intuition

> The intuitive mind is a sacred gift and the rational
> mind is a faithful servant. We have created a society
> that honors the servant and has forgotten the gift.
> —Albert Einstein

The next word in the title is *intuition*. *Intuition* brings up similar words to those raised about the *heart*: awareness, listening to the soul, and being true to self. Intuition is also an important word and plays an essential role in life decisions.

When I was working on my master's degree in social work, one of the study groups I participated in brought up topics of awareness, diaphragmatic breathing, and quieting the thoughts. In our discussions, the group began to realize that quieting the mind, listening to the heart, and using our own higher powers and awareness helped make a difference. I believe that intuition is helpful in many ways, including with internal awareness. Intuition is a process that gives us the ability to know something directly without analytic reasoning.[4] It often presents us with insight into the next direction or choice to make. If we are open to quieting the mind or thoughts, becoming more aware of what we feel, hear, sense, and know, then our own awareness may heighten and present new insight.

However, this is different from using logical and analytical thinking. In our study group, we began to realize that using both the analytical mind and intuition often enhanced our internal awareness, which presented the best answers for each of us. This brings us back to the topic of intuition and self-awareness.

As the group continued to process, we decided that intuition often guides us in finding our true answers, and we named it our barometer or thermometer. Some of the people in the group were able to identify it as a physical sensation, such as a fluttering in the stomach, which created an uncomfortable feeling that needed to be recognized. This led us back to insight and understanding, as the group realized the value of intuition.

Have you ever been driving down the street and felt something unusual guiding you to get off that street? One of the group members said she was driving down Broadway and felt uncomfortable about

---

[4] Francis Cholle, "What Is Intuition, and How Do We Use It?," Psychology Today, accessed October 30, 2022, https://www.psychologytoday.com/us/blog/the-intuitive-compass/201108/what-is-intuition-and-how-do-we-use-it.

staying on it. She remembered our discussion and chose to drive down another street to get to class. When she arrived at class, the teacher said there was construction on Broadway and several students would be late. She talked about this in the group and was prideful in listening to her thoughts and feelings and avoiding the construction. This is just one example of using intuition.

Another example is from when I was a school social worker in Arizona for twenty-seven years. In 1991, I was working in a school district in Phoenix, Arizona. School social workers in the district kept documentation and each had a locked file cabinet to keep the paperwork. One day after school, a father was angry about a situation, and he approached me in my office. I became uncomfortable with his words, body language, and facial response. I felt something inside of me say, "Get a barrier between him and you." I stepped behind my desk, called 9-1-1, and staff members came in immediately. I believe it was my intuition, a feeling of being threatened, and my internal awareness that guided me to make this decision and not panic. Because of this, I protected others and myself. This is another example of intuition, listening to your inner voice, evaluating the situation, and making the best choice at the time.

In a study conducted at the University of Missouri Columbia, Sarah A. Ward and Laura King defined intuition "or 'gut instinct' [as] the ability to understand something immediately, without the need for conscious reasoning."[5]

Transformation

> Transformation literally means going beyond your form.
> —Dr. Wayne Dyer

The last word in the title is *transformation*. Transformation relates to words such as growth, insight, learning, and change. I often compare transformation to the amazing cycle of a butterfly.

The process begins with a tiny caterpillar growing and transforming in a cocoon. Finally, it must break free from this cocoon to gain the strength to become a beautiful butterfly. There is a story about an individual who decided to help the butterfly escape from the cocoon and make the transition easier. Although this person acted out of kindness, the butterfly suffered, and one wing was neither developed nor strong. The butterfly was unable to experience the struggle and accomplishment of breaking out of the cocoon. For the remainder of the butterfly's life, the wing was smaller and weaker. In the end, the

---

[5] University of Missouri-Columbia, "People Who Rely on Their Intuition Are, at Times, Less Likely to Cheat," Science Daily, posted November 24, 2015, https://www.sciencedaily.com/releases/2015/11/151124143502.htm.

butterfly never had an opportunity to accomplish the task on its own and continued to struggle with the wing throughout its life.

On the other hand, did the butterfly really struggle? Maybe the butterfly was stronger than any other butterfly because of its determination, strength, and will to accomplish its tasks as a butterfly. Perhaps because of this change or transition, the butterfly accomplished more in its life than other butterflies, or gained additional strength due to the modifications it made to ensure its own survival. The author of this story is unknown, but credit needs to be given to the author for the parable and its usefulness in learning.

There are times when people in our lives work to rescue another person. They often do not want this individual to suffer or experience pain. However, it is important to understand that each of us has a unique path, journey, life lessons, and destination. Without experiencing our own journeys, we may instead suffer and not learn the life lessons that are necessary for our own paths and individual successes. In addition, the person rescuing is not helping but potentially sabotaging the other person's growth and learning.

Many years ago, I was working at a middle school. A student at the school often made poor choices and the law became involved. The parents were very angry and upset at their adolescent for those poor choices. The student suffered consequences imposed by the court. However, the parents worked to get their child out of trouble and to avoid the consequences. Their child did not experience consequences; therefore, that child learned that when a person does something wrong, someone will help get that person out of trouble. Years later, when the adolescent became an adult, this individual served jail time due to more poor choices. However, this time there was no one to rescue this person, and no parent to fix it or make it go away. There was only accountability and responsibility for those actions. Was the rescue helpful for this individual? The answer is probably no.

Maybe if this student had experienced the consequences when young, or participated in counseling and parenting classes, those poor choices would not have been repeated.

Now back to transformation. I compare transformation to the life cycle. It is circular. People complete different developmental tasks and move forward, transforming to the next stages in their lives.

When I worked at Phoenix Children's Hospital many years ago, I remember a doctor telling a story to the staff. He spoke about infancy, development, and the life cycle. The doctor described the stages of pregnancy and the development of the egg and sperm as they united and changed over the course of forty weeks. He discussed details and stated that at any time during those forty weeks of development, complications could occur. If there were complications during those forty weeks, an infant could be born early. If this occurred, the development of a specific stage or task could be compromised or create problems for the baby.

The doctor went on with his story and said that as an infant grows, it gains strength in its entire body. For example, the neck muscles strengthen and the infant lifts its head. Then the infant begins to roll over, starts to crawl, learns to stand, and eventually begins to walk. The doctor said that in adolescent development, there are as many stages and changes that occur as there are in an infant's first two years of life. The adolescent transitions through puberty, experiencing changes in physical, mental, social, and emotional development. This is the same in infant development; however, often the adolescent is not as cute in his or her transitions. The doctor laughed and said, "Welcome to adolescence."

These two stories help to explain a little bit about the developmental process in the life cycles of infancy and adolescence, as well as the struggles and accomplishments. This brings us back to the word *transformation*.

In my first pregnancy, I became high risk, was on bed rest, given medications, and hospitalized many times. At thirty-three weeks, my water broke, and my baby was on its way. I remember the overwhelming feelings as the staff rushed to the emergency delivery room. At one level, I was so proud of myself for helping my baby to grow inside of me for thirty-three weeks while hospitalized. However, I clearly understood that pregnancy was forty weeks and I was petrified. I remember the doctors praising me for helping the baby get to this developmental level.

I also remember the fear that gripped me in that moment, as I thought, *Will my baby be okay? What about development? What about my baby's health?* I began to pray and knew that it was now in G-d's hands. I had done the best I could do.

When a baby is developing in utero, the infant gains skills for life. Around thirty-four weeks, the infant gains the sucking and swallowing reflex skill. This aids the baby when he or she suckles or nurses.

The next thing I remember is that the experience was quick and intense—and then my baby was born.

During my pregnancy, I had strong feelings and many dreams that my baby was a boy. However, everyone around me was telling me it was going to be a girl. If my child were born a boy, it would be the first in three generations in our family. Many people continued to say repeatedly that it was a girl and I needed to realize and accept this. I had two ultrasounds: one revealed it was a girl and the other was inconclusive.

I felt I was having a boy, continued to have dreams of a boy, but stopped talking about it to others. I knew deep in my soul that I was having a boy. It became easy to doubt myself and people became concerned that I would struggle with the birth of a girl. I knew that, no matter what, all would be good as long as my baby was healthy.

My favorite OB-GYN walked in about two minutes before the baby was born, and then miracles began as the pain and excitement overtook me and my first child was born. Because of the high-risk pregnancy, there were about fifteen specialists in the room: interns, nurses, a neonatologist, and other specialists. As I cried out while pushing, one of the interns said, "Look it's a girl." Then another one said, "Are you nuts, that's a boy." My son was born.

I remember they placed him on my belly one minute and then whisked him away to the Neonatal Intensive Care Unit (NICU) for his medical care. There were so many challenging moments during that three-week period. For instance, we remember watching while two surgeons were arguing in front of his incubator. He was lying there with tubes and equipment, and they were arguing about a pending surgery, which fortunately did not happen. The early birth created a struggle for both of us. He spent three and a half weeks in the NICU for many reasons.

Another area that challenged both of us was feeding. He had not developed the sucking and swallowing reflex and had difficulty with eating and nourishment. We worked on this together with a lactation specialist. Although she was terrific, the experience was both frustrating and emotional for both of us. Weeks later, after intensive care, medical care, and physician's decisions, we were truly blessed when he was discharged home.

It was so exciting to leave the hospital with our infant. However, due to a high white cell count, we returned to the PICU (Pediatric Intensive Care Unit) two weeks later. Eventually, we left the hospital and worked with specialists in hematology and cardiology. The journey involved fear, emotions, and the unknown. Fortunately, most of the doctors were fabulous and assisted him with care in both inpatient and outpatient procedures.

The best part of the story is that although filled with heartache, emotions, learning, and growing, our child did well. Today he is an adult, giving back to others in many ways. This includes working at Make-A-Wish, granting wishes for children who have critical illnesses, and many other things to make a difference in other people's lives.

This story illustrates many components of development, transformation, and the many struggles and accomplishments individuals can experience. In addition, it speaks about intuition, knowing, and my feelings that my baby was a boy. This was twenty-eight years ago, and my son is an amazing, healthy, and blessed man. Daily, I thank G-d for my intuition, transformation, and our first-born son.

Spirituality

You must find the place inside yourself where nothing is impossible.

—Deepak Chopra

Another word associated with intuition and transformation is *spirituality*. This word may bring many thoughts and feelings. Laura Delagran quotes Dr. Christina Puchalski, director of the George Washington Institute for Spirituality and Health, as saying "that spirituality is the aspect of humanity that refers to the way individuals seek and express meaning and purpose and their connectedness to the moment, to self, to others, to nature, and to the significant or sacred."[6] In the same article, Delagran writes, "Spirituality is a broad concept with room for many perspectives. In general, it includes a sense of connection to something bigger than ourselves, and it typically involves a search for the meaning in life. As such, it is a universal human experience—something that touches us all."[7]

When I speak of spirituality, I believe it is important to honor all people's beliefs, as long as they are not harmful to the self or others. There is no right and wrong; it depends on each individual. The words that come to mind when speaking about spirituality are faith, belief, intuitiveness, blessings, feeling, knowing, and one my favorites, the true you.

For some, spirituality may bring up the unknown, which may elicit fear, anxiety, or worry, and can be threatening at times. I challenge you

---

[6] Qtd. in Louise Delagran, "What Is Spirituality?," University of Minnesota, accessed October 30, 2022, https://www.takingcharge.csh.umn.edu/what-spirituality.

[7] Delagran, "What Is Spirituality?" ?," University of Minnesota, accessed October 30, 2022, https://www.takingcharge.csh.umn.edu/what-spirituality.

to take a breath and continue to read, acknowledge, and grow. As we move forward, I encourage you to stay open in mind and heart, listen, feel the emotions, complete the exercises, and be true to yourself. Just allow this book to be the beginning of recognizing the uniqueness of your world, honoring who you are, and understanding the journey you choose to walk, as you continue to transform into the best you possible.

CHAPTER 2

Making Change

Be the change that you wish to see in the world.

—Mahatma Gandhi

The word *change* elicits many feelings and thoughts. However, when you actually think about this word and its meaning, you realize change happens constantly with people, business, nature, and the world.

One example is the changes that happen to a tree. Let's say you decide to plant a tree. You evaluate the placement of the tree. You determine where the sun will reach it, the best place to plant it, and what the tree will need for survival and growth. You prepare the earth to make it healthy for growth. You plant the seeds and water them every other day. You continue to watch the seeds as they sprout and grow, getting bigger and stronger. The roots are the foundation of this tree's life. You think for a moment, *My goodness, this tree has a foundation, and it needs me to care for it as it takes root and begins to grow.*

The tree flourishes and the trunk grows stronger, with branches budding and the leaves or pine needles blooming. The tree continues its progress, changing, growing, and becoming a full-grown tree, providing beauty and shade.

Change is evident almost daily in the tree, and can be the same for all of us. However, we often shy away from change, worried that change will be a hard struggle, a different experience, that at times brings both anxiety and worry. If we change our thinking and begin to see things differently, then we begin to see change in a positive light and as less threatening. This is the beginning of positive thinking, redirection of thought, and the process of making positive change.

I want to begin with you. See yourself as unique and different, and as someone who wants to make change. See yourself taking a step forward with a new look on life, a new journey, and a new vision. This is often the beginning of change.

In my career as a clinical social worker and therapist, I often hear people talk negatively about themselves. I am not sure when people began to feel less than, or not special, or underappreciated. It is possible you may be experiencing negative thinking and negative self-talk; however, it is important to be aware that anyone can begin changing this from negative to positive.

Where do we begin when we feel lost or not in the right place? Where do we start when that path is not giving us what we want and need? Many people have experienced hardship and trauma in their lives and this can be very wearing. With so many traumas in the world, it is challenging to see another way, a new path, or a new direction to take in life. However, the beginning is to acknowledge and honor who you are. I know it might sound "fluffy," but really think about the amazing you. It starts with a desire to change, to acknowledge that we want something different, and to step forward to make a change, even with baby steps.

You are a gift, a miracle, and a special individual. There is no one else exactly like you and that in itself makes you a miracle. You have strengths, beauty, intellect, and awareness. You are a blessing. Honor the true you, even if you are blank and cannot think of anything special about who you are. Just sit quietly and allow yourself to get out of your head and into your heart.

There will always be areas we need to work on, but for now, just sit still in a quiet and calming place, and take a few minutes to think about you. Go back in time and think about something special about you. It is time to honor yourself.

CHAPTER 3

Begin to Define Change: Our Unique Organs and Integration

Stay focused, go after your dreams and

keep moving towards your goals.

—LL Cool J

It was my sophomore year at Coronado High School in Scottsdale, Arizona. I felt like I did not belong and did not fit in. I remember thinking to myself, *I am tired of feeling this way.*

I was tired of allowing others to make me feel as if I was not special. I decided at that time that it was enough and I was making a permanent change. I was clear that the change would not be easy, but I knew in my heart that it was well worth it. I made a commitment at that moment to stop allowing the negative thoughts to spin; I would work on myself, no longer allowing other people's thoughts to be in my head. I would get out of my head and into my heart, work to become free of negativity, and give myself permission to be true to myself, be true to me.

This is when I created my new nickname: Ms. Bizarre. I began to dress as I wanted, to say what I wanted, and work harder, no longer allowing others to get into my head. Instead, I stayed in my heart, allowing myself to feel the emotions, listen to my thoughts, and be genuine in who I was.

Change is imperative in our lives. Although it can provoke a nervous energy, change does not have to be bad. We must acknowledge that. As I sat and thought about the impact I was allowing others to have in my life, I created an action plan called The A to Z Plan, which is discussed later.

Making change in life can be a challenge. We avoid this to keep things the same, even when we know it is no longer best for us. For example, I was recently talking with my son about toxic relationships. We spoke about how many people stay in toxic relationships for many reasons, such as their own previous experience, trauma, or the fear of moving forward. What people often do not recognize is the harm that relationship may cause them, even in the future. This, of course, brings us right back to honoring who we are, recognizing our uniqueness, and not allowing anyone to have the ability to make us feel less than.

The beginning of change is to identify the goal. The goal provides all of us wonderful new opportunities for change. It can help us redirect to something new, expand what we have, or finalize the next step. It can be the next stepping stone to our success.

However, there are times in our lives when we begin to doubt who we are, where we are going, and what we want in our lives. This may be because of past experiences in our lives or the put-downs, the mean-spirited negative comments, or things we have heard, felt, lived, and internalized on our paths. Therefore, the time is now. It's time to make change, to identify the value of you and what makes you unique and important.

The first question to ponder is this: Am I in my head or my heart? You may be thinking, *What does that mean?* It is one of my many mottos. Each of us is blessed with an intellect, and an incredible brain that provides us with thoughts, ideas, learning, growth, and analytical thinking.

Initially, I decided to write about the importance of the brain. However, as I began to research and write, I realized this is not my specialization, and that you, the reader, can decide how much or little you would like to be educated in this area.

The important component for me became understanding the two hemispheres and the research behind the studies of this aspect of the brain. The research I identified began back in the 1800s and continues to the present day. When I teach visualization as a tool, I explain that although the brain is a complex organ, I want the individual to understand there are two hemispheres that control the mind and body. One is more analytical, logical, and thought oriented, and the other one is creative, artistic, and imaginative.[8] Then we discuss identifying a safe place in the mind to go when imagining and relaxing. This is the beginning of the visualization process I teach, and most individuals feel benefits from it. Please take time to do your own research and decide if this is something you wish to learn more about. Details of diaphragmatic breathing and visualization will be shared in this book.

I have also worked with people who have had an accident, head trauma, stroke, or some type of brain injury. When a person experiences an injury to the brain, the outcome and recovery depends on the extent of the injury and the intensity. Since the right side of the brain controls movement and sensation on the left side of the body and the left side of the brain controls movement and sensation on the right side of the body, life after head trauma can be very different. Once again, please investigate this area, if you want to gain more knowledge. There is extensive research continuing in all areas of medical care.

I have worked with many clients who have suffered some type of brain injury. This can include mild to life-changing symptoms. Many of these individuals may experience confusion, aphasia, and problems with balance. They may also experience symptoms such as memory loss,

---

[8] Psychology Notes HQ, "The Two Hemispheres of Our Brain," The Psychology Notes HQ, posted February 14, 2020, https://www.psychologynoteshq.com/brainhemispheres/.

speech and movement concerns, decreased physical abilities, or other areas of change.

These individuals strive to work with many specialists[9] that may include, but are not limited to, neurologists, movement specialists, physical, occupational, and speech therapists, social workers, psychologists, and counselors. In addition, many people experience emotional concerns and seek psychiatric support, therapeutic counseling, and other resources that may be helpful in the healing process. As we discussed above, sometimes even with these injuries to the brain, situations may improve, or the brain may have the ability to adapt and change.

In the early 1990s, I worked as a school social worker in middle schools. One of the students I worked with participated in the special education classes at the school. This student experienced many seizures daily, and this created hardship for both her and her family. They were constantly working with multiple physicians, specialists, neurologists, and neurosurgeons to find answers to make this devastating situation stop.

I remember the teachers and family talking about working with a neurosurgeon who might be able to slow or stop the seizures by the removal of some of the hemisphere on one side of the brain. It was scary to think that they would remove some of her brain or part of a

---

[9] Mayo Clinic Staff, "Traumatic Brain Injury," Mayo Clinic, posted February 4, 2021, https://www.mayoclinic.org/diseases-conditions/traumatic-brain-injury/diagnosis-treatment/drc-20378561.

hemisphere. This student underwent the operation and recovered very well. The amazing thing was that the student returned to the school not only seizure-free but also saying and doing things no one had predicted. The family often said they felt very appreciative of the medical team. They also thought this happened because the other half of the brain took over and compensated. I will never know what happened in her brain or what the hemispheres did or did not do. I am sure that this young child had a new life. Her brain appeared to adapt to new things, and she began a new life with no more seizures. Her smiles brightened, she laughed more often, and she had a new direction. This was an amazing blessing for this child, her family, and the people who loved her.

To summarize, we are fortunate that scientists, researchers, and medical specialists continue to work to understand this complex and unique organ that we call the brain. Although the brain is one of our many gifts, sometimes it is difficult to get out of our heads and move into our hearts. It is important to begin to focus on our feelings and emotions. Oftentimes, individuals may shy away from their feelings. It can be frightening to open up about how we truly feel and see ourselves as vulnerable. However, our feelings and emotions give us incredible insight into identifying who we are, what we need, and the next direction to move forward. This brings us to the next topic of vulnerability—letting our true selves be known and seen. Okay, take a breath and let us move to the next section—you guessed it, vulnerability.

CHAPTER 4

Vulnerability: It is Part of Who We Are

There can be no vulnerability without risk; there can be

no community without vulnerability; there can be no

peace, and ultimately no life, without community.

—M. Scott Peck

Fear paralyzed me. I struggled to catch my breath and my hands were shaking. I had been sitting on the couch with my friend and her baby was sleeping in the back room. It was late at night, the drapes were closed, and we were sitting in her apartment talking. Suddenly, we heard rattling coming from the glass arcadia door. The door was locked, or so I thought. Suddenly, somebody was entering the apartment. We ran to the back room to shield the baby and locked the door. It was terrifying. It was her husband, who was trying to scare us to see how we would react if somebody broke into the house. Well, you can imagine what we had to say to him. As the fear gripped us, then the realization that we were safe overtook us, tears began to fill our eyes and we cried out, "What are you doing? That was so scary." We thought we were safe, but realized how vulnerable we really were.

Vulnerability is a word that often elicits fear, a desire to shut down, or withdraw. It is a feeling of being completely exposed, with little to no protection. No wonder people do not want to be vulnerable. It is also the ability to be open and honest. To allow you to become the best version of yourself with time and growth. Vulnerability is typically viewed as negative. According to Kira M. Newman, "a new study suggests we judge ourselves more harshly than others do."[10]

However, in this book, we will work to view vulnerability in a positive light for the process of learning and growing in yourself. We all wear our security blankets, whether we realize it or not. They are the blankets that cover our wounds and secrets that we keep from the world. What we fail to realize is vulnerability leads to more internal strength than we ever thought we had.

Each one of us has an amazing amount of internal strength, a gift that is often underappreciated. It is important to look at your whole self. We often avoid evaluating ourselves physically, mentally, socially, and emotionally. However, reflecting on who we are and where we are going will always be helpful in life.

---

[10] Newman, K.M. (2018) *Why is it so hard to be vulnerable?*, *Greater Good*. Available at: https://greatergood.berkeley.edu/article/item/why_is_it_so_hard_to_be_vulnerable.

Feelings and emotions are often an area that brings vulnerability to the surface. Being open and truthful with our feelings, being exposed, and letting our guards down at times may increase vulnerability. However, by allowing ourselves to feel, acknowledge, and experience growth and understanding, our practice of vulnerability can begin. In her book *The Power of Vulnerability: Teachings of Authenticity, Connection, and Courage*, Dr. Brené Brown focuses on the courage it takes to be vulnerable. She states, "When we dare to drop the armor that protects us from feeling vulnerable, we open ourselves to the experiences that bring purpose and meaning to our lives."[11]

We start with feelings. There is an assumption that most people are aware of and understand feelings; however, I have found that this may not be correct. The question becomes whether people really know and understand their true and real feelings and what they experience inside their bodies. I see this every day with clients as we explore the topic of feelings. Feelings are the emotional states we experience that give a sense of meaning and understanding in our lives. It can be easy to read emotions at times on our faces, in our eyes, on our mouths, and in our bodies. We physically and emotionally experience them.

One exercise I challenge clients with in session is to quickly identify as many feelings as possible in one minute with no help. The client

---

[11] Brené Brown, *The Power of Vulnerability: Teachings of Authenticity, Connection, and Courage*, read by Brené Brown, Boulder, CO: Sounds True, 2012, audiobook, 6 hr., 30 min.

typically would come up with the following feelings: sad, depressed, angry, and happy. Most people were able to identify between three and five feelings in one minute. Feeling identification is one of the many important tools that we work on together.

Frequently when I work with clients on their emotions, I might begin with a visual example, such as a cooking pot. In the pot is water. The water symbolizes the stillness of the emotion. Then we turn on the stove, initially on low, and begin to see the steam and little baby bubbles. This describes the emotion of being angry. Then the temperature is increased, and the little baby bubbles grow to larger bubbles, demonstrating an increase in the intensity of the emotion. In this visual exercise, we then place the lid on the boiling pot and the turn the burner to high. The water boils rapidly, seeps over the edge of the pot, and eventually forces the lid off the pot. This is the cycle of anger and rage.

We must acknowledge that feelings can be overwhelming. While there are times we try to avoid our emotions, this next exercise will allow you to find out more about yourself, begin self-reflection, and a better understanding of yourself.

*****Exercise*****

Please do the following.

1. Find a piece of paper, and number the lines on it from one to twenty.

2. Now, without looking anywhere—no books, no internet, no conversation with others—write down twenty feelings.

3. Write the definition of each feeling. Please take your time.

4. Concentrating on the eyes and mouth, write the facial response that demonstrates each of these feelings.

5. Identify and write down the body language that demonstrates these feelings.

6. Write a time you experienced that feeling anytime in your life.

Here is an example

1. Feeling: Happy

   - Definition: energy, a pep in your step, a feeling that things are good.

   - Facial Awareness: the eyes are bright, there is a smile, and the mouth goes up.

   - Body Awareness: the body is tall, lifted, and standing.

   - Time I felt happy: I felt happy when my friend and I were spending time at the beach.

Ask yourself a question: Why do you think feeling identification is important?

_____

_____

_____

_____

Emotional awareness assists us in identifying what we are feeling in our bodies. Feelings and emotions are special parts of each of us. Having the ability to identify the feelings we experience and understand the effects that each emotion has on us as individuals is the beginning of being true to ourselves. This first exercise will assist you in understanding feelings and emotions in a more specific way. It will allow you to be real, truthful, and genuine, and be open to vulnerable feelings, thoughts, and situations.

As discussed previously, vulnerability may create fear. However, it is a wonderful opportunity to grow and learn. It takes courage to dive in and evaluate who we are, why we are feeling these emotions, and acknowledge the specialness we each have.

There are so many feeling charts. Below is one I have created for you. On the next page is a pie chart. Please identify thirty-three positive feelings and fill in the blanks on the next page. Then choose ten positive feelings and a color that represents the word to you. Color in the chart and have fun!

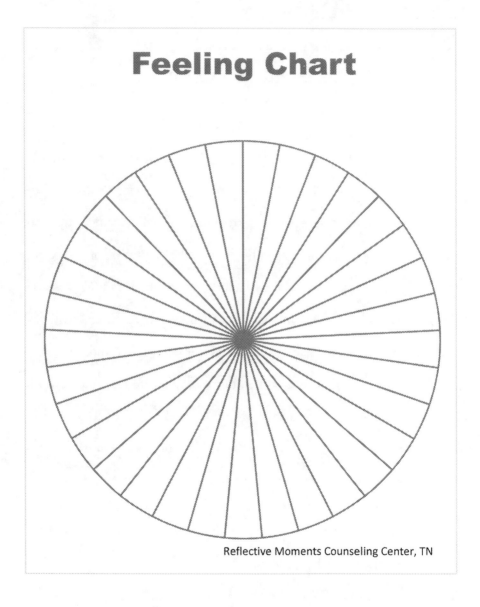

Feeling Chart

Reflective Moments Counseling Center, TN

Happy	Sadness	Jealous
Elated	Disappointed	Humiliated
Surprised	Discouraged	Pessimistic
Ecstatic	Hopeless	Bashful
Appreciated	Helpless	Weak
Hopeful	Depressed	Glad
Joyful	Lonely	Successful
Loved	Melancholy	Grateful
Excited	Confused	Pretty
Cheerful	Critical	Frightened
Satisfied	Mad	Shocked
Pleased	Frustrated	Eager
Merry	Angry	Energetic
Terrific	Irritated	Bored
Confident	Distant	Respected
Warm	Agitated	Valued
Peaceful	Resentful	Shocked
Optimistic	Guilty	Enthusiastic
Amazed	Fearful	Affectionate
Trusting	Embarrassed	Passionate
Curious	Scared	Grief
Vulnerable	Stressed	Positive
Adoring	Rejected	Negative
Proud	Busy	Sleepy
Busy	Anxious	Sick
Content	Bitter	Silly
Interested	Hurt	Calm
Playful	Threatened	Overwhelmed
Powerful	Insecure	Brave
Thrilled	Tired	Helpful
Pretty	Insecure	Encouraging
Beautiful	Nervous	Numb

The Unknown of Fear and Vulnerability

Vulnerability is not winning or losing. It's having the courage

to show up when you can't control the outcome.

—Brené Brown

It is an amazing blessing to be pregnant and have a child. The process is not always what we predict. My second son was also born with medical challenges. Due to these concerns, he experienced multiple surgeries, which required inpatient hospitalization, outpatient follow-ups, medications, and equipment that we needed training to use. I never studied nursing and did not know how to work with an IV or catheter. The nurses were supportive and encouraging, letting us know that it would be okay.

My baby lay there in the hospital and the doctor started talking about surgery. I froze, thinking, *But he is just a baby.* How do you react when the unexpected happens? How do you react when you hear something that completely throws you off and you think to yourself, *What now?*

I remember taking a breath and beginning self-talk, encouraging myself to keep breathing. That was my thought when I heard for the first time that my baby would have to have surgery. In his life, my son has endured ten surgeries with two different surgeons. Each surgery provoked many emotions, which of course included fear, panic, and an overwhelming sense of anxiety. I remember the fear paralyzing me. I felt lost and overwhelmed, and did not know what to do or to whom to turn. Sometimes it was so difficult, I needed to stop, breathe, and work on calming down. How could I take his pain away? Why did this happen? When could he go home? How could I "fix it"?

He began having surgeries when he was nine months old. These surgeries continued year after year. While initially successful, they began to fail. The next thing we knew, it was time for his third surgery. Once again, initially the procedure went well. As usual, we were home, and he was beginning to heal. Due to the intensity of these procedures, he came home with medical equipment and needed special care for his healing. However, on the third day after the third surgery, my son began to have difficulty with pain and fever. We knew again that he was struggling with his healing. The catheter had stopped working and the urine began to back up into the body, creating risk and toxicity. He was only eighteen months old.

We spoke with our surgeon multiple times on the telephone that day. I listened to his recommendations and continued following through with them, but nothing seemed to work or change. As my tears and worries grew more intense, I heard the surgeon say that he was coming to the house after his last appointment. I was so happy to hear those words and so scared. I was trembling and tears filled my eyes, but I continued to pray, "Please help me to keep my son safe."

My husband and I anxiously waited until our surgeon arrived at our home. It was unbelievable that he made a house visit, and I was extremely grateful as he entered our home. He took my baby, laid him on the carpet in the bedroom area, and began to work on him. Our child was in awful pain. He was scared, and was becoming more and more ill from the toxicity. As I watched the surgeon work on him, I held my baby's hand and tears continued to fill my eyes.

Finally, after forty-five minutes, he said, "If it doesn't improve by morning, he will need another surgery. It will be an emergency surgery at the Children's Hospital again. I will schedule it first thing in the morning." At that moment, it felt as if my stomach fell, my throat closed, and I was having difficulty calming down. The fear was overwhelming. I longed to make it stop, take his pain away, and help our child. I was so afraid.

Suddenly, something inside of me changed and I had a quiet moment. I began closing my eyes to take long, slow, deep breaths. I began to pray, and listen—really listen—no longer in my head with the racing thoughts. Slowly, I took deep and concentrated breaths, thinking I needed to quiet my mind, and allow myself to feel and be in the moment. I was working on positive, direct self-talk, as I listened to my thoughts: *I need to get out of the racing thoughts, the what ifs, the fears, and the doubts.*

As I heard these words inside, I began to relax and breathe more gently. I began to allow myself to be in the present moment. All of a sudden, I received an overwhelming sense, a feeling, a knowing, a calmness that it would be okay. I was aware, had faith, and believed that all would be okay. I was clear that the surgeon was an amazing doctor and our whole family would be there to pray, support, and love our son. My husband and I acknowledged the intense feelings. They were evident by our expressions, the looks in our eyes, and our body language.

In the morning when I awoke, a feeling of gratitude and appreciation overtook me. I realized the catheter was working again. For the time being, he would be fine, and his healing began one more time. Fortunately, years later, he graduated from his annual medical checks, and now is very successful working in the music and social media industry as a content creator. We have gratitude daily and feel appreciation for his health and well-being.

Vulnerability can be very emotional and confusing. It often makes someone feel exposed and open to the unknown. Fear is the emotion we feel when our safety may be at risk; both can take us by surprise and be uncomfortable to experience. We feel paralyzed from fear, worry, and panic, as if we want to escape or leave quickly. Fleeing is not always possible and finding tools to use in these challenging situations helps to create healthy choices, stability, and future growth.

Strategies that I have found to be helpful when these emotions overtake me are to acknowledge the overwhelming feelings and say them aloud. I believe when your brain hears your voice and words, it processes the feelings differently. When we speak of fear, it may bring up many difficult feelings and thoughts. Fear maybe based on learned behaviors, past experiences, the unknown, or ongoing thoughts. Fear can affect us in many different ways. Physiologically, our hearts may race, our bodies may become clammy or sweaty, we might shake or tremble, and can move into a state of panic. None of this is enjoyable for anyone. Our thoughts may begin to race and cause an overwhelming sense of the unknown. These vulnerable feelings range on a continuum from high to low, and may cause us to be anxious, worried, or overwhelmed. Sometimes, we may experience a feeling of paralysis due to the level of fear and feel stuck in our situations.

The first and most important thing to evaluate is safety. Are there any safety concerns, anything that must be taken care of, or do you need help? I call this evaluating the Three Ss: safety, security, and stability. It is something I use in my everyday life and clinical practice.

As a crisis worker in the hospitals, I would team with the emergency doctors to assess patients who were in the emergency room. I would work alongside the physician assessing patients who were suicidal, homicidal, psychotic, or had drug and/or alcohol intoxication. I always began with my Three Ss. I encourage people to evaluate the Three Ss. If there is ever a concern for safety, stop and reach out for help.

Either call a crisis number, go to an emergency department, or call a trusted adult. If safety is ever a factor, then the most important decision becomes keeping yourself and others safe. I hope that this is not the issue for you, and we can move forward knowing all are safe. However, if safety is the case for you, or anyone else, then getting help immediately is imperative!

*****Exercise*****

Fear: How do you define fear in your life?

_____

_____

_____

_____

_____

_____

Write a list of the things that bring up fears in you. Identify the things that hold you back in life.

Examples:

A) Fear of public speaking in a college class: The assignment is to stand in front of the class and give an oral presentation. Now evaluate:

_____

_____

_____

1. How do I feel at this moment?

_____

2. What am I experiencing in my body right now?

_____

3. What are my thoughts at this moment?

_____

B) Fear of speaking up for yourself in a relationship. Now evaluate:

_____

_____

_____

1. How does it make me feel when I have something to say, but I ignore my thoughts or feelings? (example: nervousness, unworthiness)

_____

2. What would happen if I speak up in a healthy manner? (Example: "It bothers me when you say you will be home at five o'clock p.m. and do not show up until eight o'clock p.m. Can you please call next time?")

_____

3. Now it is your turn. Write a list of the fears you experience in life.

_____

_____

_____

_____

Now that you have created a list of your fears, I would like you to congratulate yourself. That is right. Good job! Now take your right hand, place it on your left shoulder, and pat yourself on the back, repeating this phrase three times aloud: "Good job me."

Okay, you can smile and laugh now. This exercise can enhance all of us. It acknowledges our accomplishments, supports us when we verbalize the words aloud, and provides our souls with acknowledgment of our successes. This is an important component in stepping forward and making changes in your life. It really is. Now that you have identified a list of fears, it is time to dive in deeper.

Example:

Fear: Making a new friend.

How does it feel to make a new friend?

Answer: nervous and worried. You may wonder if the person will like you. Okay, stay out of your head. Just sit quietly and listen to your heart, feel the emotions that are surrounding you, and allow yourself to be in the present moment of having a new friend.

*****Exercise*****

Please get a piece of paper, read each question, and then answer. Complete five of these.

1. **I feel** ....

   (**Example**: nervous, worried, shy, or anxious)

   When I ....

   (**Example:** identify the situation, such as when I meet someone new)

   Because ....

   (**Example**: I do not know if he or she will like me)

2. **I want to feel** ....

   (**Example**: confident, happy, and adventurous)

   When you ....

   (**Example:** spend time with me, play sports,)

   Because ... .

   (**Example:** you are my friend, you are fun)

3. **I want to feel** ....

   (**Example**: confident, happy, and adventurous)

When you ....

Because ... .

4. **I want to feel** ....

   (**Example**: confident, happy, and adventurous)

   When you ....

   Because ... .

   Example Goal: Making a New Friend

Introduction: Identify a place where you can meet someone, go to that place, and begin.

Example: At school. "Hi, my name is . How are you doing today? What do you like to do for fun?" Open-ended questions promote conversation better than yes or no questions. They allow someone to begin a conversation and communicate. If you want to converse with someone, it is important to stay away from yes or no questions. Initiating a conversation presents you as confident and allows you to step forward as being friendly, approachable, and kind. Most people like to have someone take an interest in them.

Sometimes in conversations, we do not listen to one another. We interrupt to ask the person a question and then turn the conversation to ourselves. Many times, we are so busy wanting to respond to the other person that we never really listen to him or her.

Beginning to learn and find out what an individual is interested in creates a discussion with commonality. If the new person is welcoming to you, continue the conversation. If the individual is less responsive to you, then be proud of your accomplishment and do not personalize his or her response. Move forward and begin again with someone new and approachable. Repeat the process and be prideful. You have stepped forward and accomplished your goal.

Now repeat an earlier exercise: Put your hand on your shoulder and say aloud three time; "Good job me!" Congratulations on a job well done. You did it!

CHAPTER 5

Quiet the Head and Listen to the Heart

Have the courage to follow your heart and intuition.

They somehow already know what you truly want

to become. Everything else is secondary.

—Steve Jobs

Stress may be both emotional and physical in the body. This may happen due to anticipating a situation or experiencing it. As the stress increases, you feel it physically, mentally, and emotionally in your body. In addition, stresses in life can be both positive and negative. Some examples of positive stress include getting married, having a baby, and taking a new job.

Alternatively, negative stress may include the loss of a job, developing an illness, or a friend moving away. All of these events will bring changes in life.

Learning strategies of coping and knowing ways to handle life experiences assists people in daily living. There are both healthy and unhealthy coping tools and finding healthier ways to manage stress is the beginning of making positive changes in one's life. Knowing and understanding ways to make positive choices, calm yourself, reduce racing thoughts, and use healthy coping skills in life continues throughout this book.

As discussed earlier, the brain is an amazing organ that is constantly busy thinking, processing, and learning. According to Remez Sasson, the average person experiences approximately 2,500 to 3,500 thoughts an hour, and between 60,000 and 80,000 thoughts per day.[12] Our brains are very busy, and it can be difficult to quiet the thoughts. Many of these thoughts are not important and are words, phrases, and thoughts repeating multiple times. These thoughts may also be negative and become overwhelming as they race in our minds. This can be overpowering, and people may begin to spin in their thoughts, experience-racing thoughts, analyze the thoughts, and overthink them. At times, this may create increased feelings of being overwhelmed and may bring fears and anxiety forward.

As the title states, get out of your head and into your heart. This strategy becomes helpful in finding ways to quiet the mind and

---

[12] Remez Sasson, "How Many Thoughts Does Your Mind Think in One Hour?" Success Consciousness, accessed October 3, 2022, https://www.successconsciousness. com/blog/inner-peace/how-many-thoughts-does-your-mind-think-in-one-hour.

experience a sense of calmness. With thoughts racing, our minds spinning, and often our anxiety rising, working to quiet the mind and slow down the thoughts takes commitment and dedication. This is the beginning of getting out of your head and into your heart. As we continue our journey together, take your time exploring the many tools and resources and building your own toolbox.

One of the many strategies I use in therapy to assist clients is diaphragmatic breathing and body awareness. Anyone can accomplish this with time and practice. Here is the tool.

Sit quietly and begin to experience body awareness. Recognize the feelings inside, quiet the thoughts, and focus on the breath. Listen to your heart, and continue quieting the mind. This is a process sometimes called meditation, mindfulness, and redirecting your head to your heart. At times, you may feel challenged by meditation and relaxation because of your schedule, racing thoughts, or lack of commitment to a meditation practice. However, by creating a routine, practicing, and implementing this in your daily life, the mind, body, and spirit align.

There are many, books, articles, apps, podcasts, and online tools. These offer education in and strategies for teaching the importance of meditation, supporting the idea of calming the body, understanding the awareness of breath, and using visualization and relaxation to reduce stress.

The study of mindfulness is not a new concept, despite what some might think. Mindfulness is a practice that many use and benefit from.

You may want to explore the many tools and techniques that assist in mindfulness and implement the best strategy for you.

Remembering that this is not about right and wrong, but the best fit for you. Psych.com has an article listing the top twenty-five best meditation resources.[13]

Another intervention that I often use is visualization. We are fortunate to have creative minds that allow us to imagine. We can use our imagination, think about past memories, look at pictures, or identify places to visit in person or in our minds. Allowing our imagination and creativity to assist in the relaxation process provides an opportunity for an escape into peaceful moments. Closing our eyes and bringing an image forward in our minds is a part of visualization exercises. Imagining shapes, beauty, color, calmness, and scenes is often like creating a picture or a movie in our minds.

There are many ways to use this technique; however, the one I often use involves thinking of a place that feels safe, calm, and peaceful. You may have been there before, seen it on TV, looked at it in a magazine, or imagined it. Places I often use in my mindfulness activities are in nature. I think about the forest, the beach, or a waterfall. Below is an exercise to take you on a journey of mindfulness. Sit back, breathe gently, and enjoy your moments of relaxation.

[13] Carolyn Fagan, "Top 25 Best Meditation Resources and Guided Meditation Apps," Psycom, accessed October 28, 2022, https://www.psycom.net/mental-health-wellbeing/meditation-resources.

*****Exercise*****

Find a place that is quiet and where you feel safe, secure, and calm. Inside or outside is fine, but if you are able to find a place outside with nature, sometimes that may be more calming and peaceful.

1. Allow yourself to sit and commit to work on this exercise for ten to twenty minutes. However, if you can only start with five minutes, it is not a problem. In time, with practice and commitment, people often gain the ability to relax and become calmer, clearer in their thinking, more focused, and able to redirect negative thinking to positive thinking.

2. Now that you are seated and quiet, please begin the exercise. Place your hand gently on your abdomen above your belly button. Begin to breathe gently and calmly. Use your breath by inhaling at a slow count of four through your nose. With the breath, push your belly out, make it big, as if you were blowing up a balloon in your belly, and push the air out gently and slowly. Now use your breath and breathe out through the mouth. Continue to practice the slow breath in a relaxed state.

3. This breath uses the diaphragm and is often called diaphragmatic breathing. I believe it is one of the most relaxed breaths used. Many professions use this breathing technique, including

martial arts, public speaking, dancing, singing, performing, and of course, meditation. Please be aware that it is a gentle, relaxed breath. The goal is not to be thinking about the breath, but utilizing it, slowly, calmly, and in a relaxed manner.

There are many articles which discuss the importance of the diaphragm and the breath. When I teach diaphragmatic breathing, I stress the importance of the belly and the breath that is taken in slowly and gently, and then released the same way. This technique is research-based both in mindfulness and health wellness.

Diaphragmatic breathing is meant to help you use the diaphragm correctly while breathing. The breathing technique offers several benefits to your body including reducing your blood pressure and heart rate and improving relaxation.[14] Research studies continue in the area of breath work and the many benefits it has on the whole person. Honoring yourself and implementing a daily routine can be a great beginning in making change.

---

[14] Cleveland Clinic, "Diaphragmatic Breathing," Cleveland Clinic, accessed October 30, 2022, https://my.clevelandclinic.org/health/articles/9445-diaphragmatic-breathing.

***** **Exercise** *****

Find a comfortable chair to sit in, uncross your arms and legs, keep your feet on the floor, and close your eyes. Begin by taking a slow, deep breath. Imagine a special place in your mind. Some may see color and an image, while others see dark colors and/or nothing. Either way, there are no worries—just use your imagination, relax, and work on quieting the mind. If this becomes overwhelming, go back to the breath and focus on breathing in and out in a gentle and calming manner.

Close your eyes and begin to slow your breathing, even slower, and slower, breathing in through the nose to a count of four and slowing the breath. Focus on the preciousness of the breath. Think about your belly, right above your belly button, near the diaphragm. Continue to pretend there is a balloon in your belly; with the breath, blow the balloon up. This gives a more relaxed and concentrated breath. Now just forget about the balloon and quietly and gently breathe. Remember to give it five to twenty minutes. Just relax and breathe.

If you choose to implement visualization, use your imagination and think about a calm and peaceful picture in your mind. See the color, image, shape, beauty, and calmness. Breathe slowly and steadily in a relaxed and calm way. If at any time thoughts enter your mind, quietly think, *Thank you for the thought*, and return to the breath. Just breathe.

Think about people who participate in martial arts, yoga, or dance, or who sing, play an instrument, or perform in theater. These people are aware of their diaphragms and the necessity of using the diaphragm to its full potential. Now it is your turn. As you continue to breathe in and out slowly, relax deeply with no worries. Enjoy your time. Practice and find what works for you. However, remember that although the breath is important, it is not the focus; quieting the mind is the true focus.

One day, I treated myself to a special massage at a resort in Scottsdale, Arizona. When I walked into the room, there was this beautiful, small basket hanging on the wall. The massage therapist stated, "It's time for you to relax, but before you get ready, think about anything that is causing you worry, and put those thoughts in the basket for now." She then gave me a few minutes to reflect on worries that I wanted to rid myself of. A few minutes later, she returned and took the basket away. This creative idea is helpful and another intervention for our toolboxes. It gives time to reflect on worries and remove any that you may be feeling. Working to remove our worries and concerns assists in feeling calmer and less stressed. Removing negative thoughts will create a space of quiet and allow a more relaxed present state. Using this before starting your diaphragmatic breathing and visualization is a key to becoming more relaxed.

Many years later, my family decided to visit one of the unique museums in Phoenix, Arizona: the Heard Museum. The Heard

Museum is filled with cultural, educational, and beautiful collections of Native American history and art.

While I wandered the museum gift shop, I was overwhelmed as I looked down to see the basket from my massage experience so many years prior. The staff told me that it was from the San Carlos Apache tribe, one of the many Native American tribes that specializes in making ceremonial baskets. This unique basket now sits in my office, adding character and beauty, and reminding me of a unique memory in my life.

***** **Exercise** *****

Another tool to add to your toolbox is writing activities. These are wonderful tools to use. There are many writing techniques such as journal writing, free writing, using prompts, and automatic writing. These tools are helpful to use whether you are a writer or not. Some of the people I work with are unable to write due to their situations. They may instead use a recorder, a computer, a phone, an app, or anything that works for them. Some of them choose to have someone write in a special notebook for them. There is no right or wrong way. Just use the resources that support and are helpful for you.

Journaling can help create more balance in life and assist in processing situations, memories, or the past, present, and future. Allowing our thoughts to get out of our heads and onto paper is often helpful. At times, this is challenging; however, using prompts, words, or phrases often assists in the process.

Free writing is a technique used by taking paper and a pen and just writing. You are not thinking, worrying about spelling or grammar— you are just writing. At times, my clients have referred to this as "barfing it up." This technique allows people to get things out of their heads and is often less threatening for many. Allowing these thoughts to no longer weigh in your head and heart often helps calm you.

Studies have found long-term benefits of all types of writing, including expressive writing for emotional health outcomes.[15] Writing tools are also helpful when people experience overwhelming thoughts and/or sleep concerns such as insomnia or excessive sleep. At times, people may feel so wound up or tight in their bodies after situations that becoming calm, sitting down, or lying down is difficult. When using these techniques, people can grant themselves permission to let go of the stressors. If someone is concerned about forgetting thoughts before they go to sleep, this will allow them to keep the thoughts on paper. Another tool to use is writing the thoughts down and taking them back in the morning, after a good night's sleep. Decreasing stress and experiencing a good night's sleep allows time for the head, heart, and body to heal and rejuvenate.

These methods assist in redirecting thoughts, gaining a true focus on self, and allowing the individual to be calm in the present moment. In addition, it provides a person with the opportunity to be independent in skills and gain more confidence.[16] They provide strategies to use with internal strength and assist a person in guiding and honoring the self.

---

[15] Karen A. Baikie and Wilhelm K. Baikie, "Emotional and Physical Health Benefits of Expressive Writing," *Advances in Psychiatric Treatment*, 11, no. 5 (September 2005): 338–346, https://doi.org/10.1192/apt.11.5.338.

[16] Ronita Mohan, "Why Learning New Skills Is Good for Your Confidence," Thrive, posted July 8, 2019, https://thriveglobal.com/stories/why-learning-new-skills-is-good-for-your-confidence/.

CHAPTER 6

Past, Present, and Future: Moments of Time

The past is behind, learn from it. The future is ahead,

prepare for it. The present is here, live it.

—Thomas Monson

I remember watching him perform magic and ventriloquism. I was the Special Project Coordinator at the Phoenix Children's Hospital. The children at the Child Developmental Preschool were in awe of the puppet talking. They began to squeal with laughter and excitement watching the man holding the talking puppet.

A year later, we met again as I volunteered to work at Camp Rainbow, a camp for children who have a diagnosis of cancer. I was a camp counselor for the adolescents and he was the Camp Director. This is also where I met a very special young person, who would change my life.

She was fifteen years of age, beautiful, funny, talented, and in remission from her cancer. That year she made a difference in so many lives with her personality, wit, and humor. Fast forward one year later and things changed drastically after camp. I found myself sitting at her bedside, holding her hand, and gazing into her eyes as she neared the end of life. I remember the overwhelming feeling of appreciation for an amazing young woman who lives on now in my heart. That day she informed me that a doctor had said she would likely not see her sixteenth birthday. As I held her hand that day, she turned to me smiling, and with wide eyes said, "I told them I would beat this. I turned sixteen yesterday and did things I wanted to do. I showed them." She died two days later but continues to shine her light from above.

Now, thirty-one years later, our lives continue to be integrated as we merge the past, present, and future together. The director of the camp (the ventriloquist performing at the preschool who sat with me at her funeral) is the one I married. We continue to share our lives together, connecting the past, present, and future. Let's continue to explore how the past, present, and future connect.

I often speak about present moments and their importance in a person's life. I also talk about the integration of the past and future and the way they all interconnected. The present moment is the moment that you are in right now. It is so easy to miss the moment of time you are actively experiencing. This moment could be about beauty, humor, learning, or just being. Life is brief, and it is easy for people to miss out if they are living in the past or moving into the future too quickly. It is very easy to miss present moments if you are not paying attention.[17]

I remember how hard it was to work three jobs, do my best to continue to be a part of the family, see my extended family, and keep up on all the necessary tasks. I felt pulled in many directions and was unable to slow down. Often, it felt as if there was no time to for me, no time to think or take care of myself, but only time for survival and completing tasks. This was a place of high emotions for me as I continued to transfer from one activity to the next. At times, it could be brutal as I raced from one job to another, came home, saw my family, and then fell asleep to begin the journey again.

After years of employment, my husband was laid off from his job; this was an emotional time. At times, he presented with immense sadness, maybe even depression, and I needed to stay supportive for him. He continued to apply for jobs daily, and at times was able to find temporary employment. We had two young children, bills to pay, and life that needed to continue. Because of this predicament, I needed to work, and I did. I worked seven days a week for eighteen months, unless I was ill.

---

[17] Paul Ratner, "New Controversial Theory: Past, Present, Future Exist Simultaneously," Big Think, accessed September 30, 2021, https://bigthink.com/hard-science/a-controversial-theory-claims-present-past-and-future-exist-at-the-same-time/.

The months continued and before we knew it, New Year's Eve had arrived. We had decided to stay in for the night. We ate great food, watched movies, and were together with the kids. I talked with both my parents earlier, saying, "Happy New Year. I look forward to seeing you and the family tomorrow." Our whole family would be together on New Year's Day spending time with one another. This was a big deal for me; the long hours I worked did not leave much time to spend with them. However, that never happened. It was late when I received a call that something had happened, and I needed to get to the hospital right away. This moment was filled with so many emotions that it was difficult to manage.

My father was one of the greatest, strongest, most loving, and honest men that I have ever known. I was very close to my dad; he was family oriented, artistic, loving, funny, very kind, professional, and a wonderful role model. He made a difference in our world. After the call, my husband and I secured our kids, and rushed to the hospital to find that things did not look good. My dad was at the end of his life, and we had to say goodbye. Even as I write this, tears are flowing, and I am allowing myself to stop and be in the present moment of sadness and loss, as I honor my feelings and thoughts, and love my father once again.

Present moments are gifts of time. Slowing down to see, hear, feel, know, and be in the moment is necessary in my life, and I hope in yours. However, this is not an easy task, as discussed previously. Sometimes the present moments are painful, sad, or so busy that slowing down is not an option—or so we think.

Thinking about present moments and living in them can be easy for some and difficult for others. Being present in moments of time is a key to balance in life. This concept often is not discussed or may be missed in everyday life. It is easy to lose track of the moment now, the moment that just passed, and the moment that you missed.

Present moments include being mesmerized by flames in a fireplace, watching a bird that glides through the sky so gracefully, hearing enduring words, watching a child take his or her first step, and feeling the warm sunshine while walking on the beach or in the forest. It is common to miss these present moments because we move so fast, live in the past, or even live in the future. However, being aware of the *now* is imperative in our lives.

An Example of Past, Present, Future

A college student enrolls in a class, and cannot wait to finish the class so that she gets the three credited hours. However, the student must enroll, pay the fee, and get the books. The student must attend the class, participate in the assignments, and turn in the assignments. In addition, she must study, take the tests, and then pass the class. The student looks forward futuristically, waiting for the class to end while not realizing that the class may contain the building blocks for the second class. Alternatively, this class may have a group project where this student will eventually meet a best friend. Maybe the professor will be an incredible teacher and inspire the student in her future studies and career. Present moments are gifts for each of us, and if we truly participate in the moments, they may surprise us, and become, precious moments in our life.

Transferring from Present Moments to Precious Moments

When I think of precious moments, I am
overwhelmed with feelings of intensity.
I realize they are unique and special moments that
are mine to keep and always remember.
—Suzi U. Wall, 01-02-2011 (Dedicated to my father)

*****Exercise*****

Create a list of present moments in your life happening now.

_____

_____

_____

What have you learned or seen in those moments?

_____

_____

_____

How do you define a precious moment? Is it when you received an award, had a child, or spent time with a special someone? -

_____

_____

_____

_____

_____

Identify five precious moments in your life and what makes them precious to you.

1.

2.

3.

4.

5.

Take a little bit of time and answer these questions.

- What do I value in my life?

_____

- What is one thing I want in my life? (Examples: abundance, health, career, family, and so on)

_____

_____

_____

_____

Now it is time to create a step-by-step guide of your past, present, and future.

1. How do your past, present, and future connect?
2. What have your choices been in the past?
3. What do you choose now in the present?
4. What do you want for the future?

- Remember to begin by identifying then creating the A to Z Plan (discussed in Chapter 8), and finally implementing the process. (If you become frustrated, then take a break, go outside, exercise, use your tools, and know it is fine to go slowly, to not have all the answers, or come back and start again later.)

- Take your time with these activities and tools and know that you can do this. It starts with believing in yourself and moving forward one-step at a time. Yes, even small steps are movement.

CHAPTER 7

Relationships in Life

When I let go of what I am, I become what I might be.

—Lao Tzu

As we sat together at the beach, enjoying a beautiful day with the sun shining, the waves filled us with beauty and calmness. We felt the sun on our shoulders, looked up and saw the beautiful blue sky with wispy clouds, and felt a sense of happiness, peace, and tranquility. We looked at one another and began to laugh, realizing the precious, present moment we had found. We had been friends for over thirty-seven years. We sat and pondered this, realizing how lucky we were to have each other in our lives. I thought to myself, *I am so fortunate to have found a friend, someone I can count on, someone I can trust in, someone I call, my friend.*

Relationships can be both wonderful and challenging. They can be both healthy and unhealthy and often teach us lessons in life.

These lessons may be about friendship, social skills, communication, socialization, emotional health, and connection to self.

There are many types of relationships: professional, social, intimate, parental, and acquaintance, to name a few. Qualities and characteristics are also important in relationships. Identifying characteristics that are important helps us know and understand what type of relationships we choose to maintain in our lives. Examples of characteristics in healthy relationships may include communication, trust, honesty, intimacy, connection, friendship, and love. For example, two people meet and establish a first impression of each other. First impressions are important, but not always the most significant part of a relationship. Most individuals enjoy connection with others.

When you first meet someone, you may begin with the attraction phase. You may see the other person physically, listen to his or her voice, hear his or her words, and maybe even laugh from the person's humor. Once there is a connection, people begin to feel more comfortable with one another and spend more time together. They learn about each other and this often brings comfort, safety, and closeness.

Each relationship has important qualities and people begin to find comfort in the connection. For example, the relationship with a supervisor is different from a friendship, which is different from an intimate partner relationship. However, all have qualities and characteristics that are important for the success of that relationship.

A popular saying, credited to both Eleanor Roosevelt and Brian A. "Drew" Chalker, is, "People always come into your life for a reason, season, and a lifetime. When you figure out which it is, you know exactly what to do."

Have you ever found that some people are in your life for a short time, maybe at work, in a neighborhood, or in a community? Then they are gone from your life. It is interesting how many lessons we can learn in our relationships. I have worked with some people who become very upset with this quotation. In processing their thoughts and feelings, they discuss the significance of the relationship and struggle with the ending. This is understandable when we care for, love, and feel connected to others, and they disappear from our lives.

Another way to look at this is the blessing you have experienced in the relationship, the tools or resources you gained, and the growth in your life. Although we may miss and love those people, we have the memories and the significant precious moments to keep.

***** **Exercise** *****

In this exercise, first we will define what a relationship is. Then we will move into identifying different types of relationships. Finally, we will create a list of relationships important to you. Why are these relationships important, what do you receive and give in the relationships, and how will you continue to work on relationships in a healthy manner?

Relationships: Examples listed below

1. Write a definition of relationships.

2. Write a list of five to ten different types of relationships.

3. Create a list of the top ten characteristics you want in a relationship.

4. Identify the important relationships in your life and then write:

   a. Why they are important; and

   b. How you both benefit from the relationship.

5. Create a list of things you can do together in the relationship.

6. How will you continue to foster this relationship and let it grow?

Example:

1. **Definition**: A relationship is a connection between two people.

2. **Types of Relationships**: professional, intimate, friendship, etc.

3. **Characteristics**: honesty, trust, communication, etc.

4. **Relationship and why it is important**: Jim is a co-worker, and is dependable, on time, and creative.

5. **Activities to do**: Work on projects, go to lunch, talk, etc.

6. **Foster the relationship**: Continue working together, spend time learning from one another, etc.

Please define what a relationship means to you.

_____

_____

_____

Identify different types of relationships. (**Examples:** parents, children, teachers, coaches, friends, etc.)

_____

_____

_____

_____

Why are relationships important to you?

_____

_____

_____

In over thirty years of working as a social worker and therapist, I have noticed that people often bring up the topic of relationships as sources of joy and also of significant stress. It is important to realize the majority of people thrive when they connect with others and acknowledge that everyone has both strengths and challenges. If we take time to really see people, listen closely, and work on being strength-based, we will often see the value in each person. This is a significant component for both the relationship and for our own personal growth.

One day, I was with another close friend. I was about twenty years old and cared for this person deeply. I could feel the pain he was experiencing and wanted to fix it. I tried to help but failed. Towards the end of the conversation, he said, "You know you can't fix this right? You can't make my pain go away for me." I heard him and understood. As much as I wanted to make it right for him, it was his journey, his lesson, and his teachable moment, and I could not fix it for him.

Control versus No Control:

Many people think that we have control over situations, people, and life. However, we really do not have control over anything except ourselves. What do we really have true control over? Is it the weather or what someone says or does? Do we have control over the grade on a paper in school? Maybe, or maybe not. The individual may research, write, study, and turn the paper in on time only to receive a lower or higher grade than expected.

I remember being in graduate school many years ago when this happened to me. I had worked very hard on a project and turned it in to the professor. When I received the grade, I was stunned. She had given the paper an 89.9 percent. I remember going to the professor and questioning why I received this grade. I was told it was not an A paper, but the professor would use it as an example for the other classes, because it was so well done. I remember my frustration as I spoke with the professor about using my paper as an example, but not giving it the grade it deserved, which I felt was an A. She said she understood, but would not change the grade. I remember my overwhelming feelings of frustration, sadness, and disappointment. I even said to her, "What if I tap dance? Will you change the grade?" The professor laughed and said, "No, the grade stands." I realized it was over, and needed to move forward, recognizing that I had no control over her decision and needed to let it go.

Life is not fair, but often teaches many lessons. We may choose a different direction or make a different choice; however, we do not have control over everything or everyone. This is a lesson I often discuss and teach called "Control versus No Control."

Think about reality and what we really have control over, and then complete the activity below.

***** **Exercise** *****

Think about the people in your life, in the community, or even in the world. It is an interesting activity as we become more accepting of what we can do and how we can make change in our personal lives. The control really lies with you, your choices, and decisions.

The two boxes below are ready for you to identify specific items you truly believe you do or do not have control over.

Control

No Control

Examples:

Control: What I say and do, who I spend time with, who my friends are, what my choices are, etc.

No Control: I have no control over anyone else, what they say or do, or their choices, etc.

The **Six Principles** I speak about in control verses no control:

1. **Listen:** you have the ability to listen to others.

2. **Guide:** you have the ability to guide others with thoughts, education, and research.

3. **Support:** you have the ability to support others.

4. **Encourage:** you have the ability to encourage others.

5. **Love:** you have the ability to love others.

6. **Be there:** you have the ability to be there for others.

Another important component of relationships is trust. *Trust* is a belief that the person is truthful, reliable, safe, and dependable. This means that what the person says is truthful and accurate. Trust—or the belief that someone can be relied on to do what the person says he or she will do—is a key element of social relationships and a foundation for cooperation.[18]

---

[18] Paul Thaguard, "What Is Trust?," *Psychology Today*, accessed October 30, 2022, https://www.psychologytoday.com/us/blog/hot-thought/201810/what-is-trust.

Erik Erikson was an ego psychologist who developed one of the most popular and influential theories of development. While his theory was impacted by psychoanalyst Sigmund Freud's work, Erikson's theory centered on psychosocial development rather than psychosexual development.[19] Erikson developed and created the eight stages of psychosocial development, a framework addressing human behavior in order to understand growth, development, and learning. The first stage in infancy is the oral sensory stage, which develops from birth through eighteen months. The important event that occurs from this stage is development of trust versus mistrust. An infant forms a special bond or connection with the caregiver by developing a sense of trust. In this stage of learning, the infant can trust the world. Touching, talking, looking, playing, singing, and caring for the infant are all components of the first cycle of trust. In infancy, the baby communicates all needs through crying. If the infant is hungry, tired, frustrated, or needs to be fed or changed, he or she communicates that through crying. If the caretaker responds quickly to the infant and meets the infant's needs, then trust begins to develop. However, when an infant feels threatened, scared, or fearful, and the infant's needs are not met, the infant begins to feel a lack of safety. Instead of building trust, mistrust begins to

---

[19] Kendra Cherry, "Erikson's Stages of Development," Verywell Mind, accessed August 3, 2022, https://www.verywellmind.com/erik-eriksons-stages-of-psychosocial-development-2795740.

develop. When mistrust develops, the infant begins to feel unsafe and lacks trust in the world, which may affect him or her throughout life.[20]

While working with children in the child protective system, I often saw attachment and bonding concerns. This is often due to their lack of trust from previous experiences and traumas. One day, I walked into a family's home and watched one of their young foster children slowly fall to the floor and curl into the fetal position. That she had experienced trauma, resulting in a lack of trust, caused me great sadness. However, as I worked with her slowly and gently, and with tools to assist with her trauma, she began to feel safe, secure, and stable—the Three Ss. It was encouraging watching her become more comfortable, connecting to her new family, and beginning to trust.

John Bowlby is widely recognized as the founder of attachment theory. He was both a psychiatrist and psychologist.[21] Bowlby recognized that on this foundation of trust and security, a child's emotional life is built and relationships are formed. Attachment is the connection and bond that someone has for another person with whom he or she has developed a relationship of safety, security, and stability in trust.

Bowlby defined attachment as a "lasting psychological connectedness

[20] Kendra Cherry, "Trust vs. Mistrust: Psychosocial Stage 1," Verywell Mind, accessed March 7, 2021, https://www.verywellmind.com/trust-versus-mistrust-2795741.
[21] Kendra Cherry, "Biography of Psychologist John Bowlby," Verywell Mind, last updated March 29, 2020, https://www.verywellmind.com/john-bowlby-biography-1907-1990-2795514.

between human beings."[22] Many theorists have paved the way in understanding behaviors, development, attachment, and growth.

Just as trust develops, mistrust also occurs. There are times when someone discovers that the trust in a relationship is broken. This often brings feelings of hurt and pain, and can leave a person feeling shattered or traumatized. Although it is possible to earn back trust in relationships, it is often very difficult and outside interventions with a counselor may be helpful.

Oftentimes individuals want to know and understand what happens when trust was broken. Many stories surround healthy and happy relationships that changed over time due to deception, lies, mistrust, and feelings that something was not right. Evaluating relationships and deciding if they are moving forward in a healthy way is important for all of us. In order for healthy relationships to continue to grow, trust is necessary. When trust has been broken, a person can feel overwhelmed, numb, angry, or sad, and as if the person has to climb out of a dark hole or up a mountain with little to no energy. Evaluating if the relationship is repairable takes great strength, commitment, and sincerity. Starting with the truth is the beginning of making changes in the relationship. Owning and being responsible for the choices that were made, the lies that were told, the deception that occurred, and stepping forward

---

[22] Kendra Cherry, "Biography of Psychologist John Bowlby."

by communicating may be the beginning of a decision to repair the relationship or not.

Sometimes one partner in the relationship is waiting for the other person to be honest and truthful, but instead secrets are learned and the situation worsens. Although knowing the truth is important, the intricate details can sometimes be helpful and other times may be more harmful. They may cause increased hurt and pain, and can make things worse.

Taking time to understand the truth, feel the emotions, talk to the person, and grieve, is important. However, sometimes people do not allow the problem to be done, completed, and over, and this is not healthy. Continuing to discuss it repeatedly and never moving forward continues the unhealthy patterns of behavior.

Starting with an investment in yourself, each other, and the relationship is often the beginning. Working on healthy choices, communication, honesty, and forgiveness are a few areas to be explored. Oftentimes it may be helpful to have a trained professional therapist to assist with this process. This involves working together to evaluate the future and rebuild healthier relationships with one another, or assist in healthy decisions for the future.

It is always important to take care of yourself, especially when stresses or traumas increase. Initially start by honoring yourself and your value. Work to sit quietly and use diaphragmatic breathing, visualization, and relaxation to calm yourself. Listen to your heart, not your head. When stresses and traumas happen, often people's thoughts spin in their minds repeatedly, anxiety rises, and stress may affect their daily lives. This is the time to work on the exercises and activities discussed earlier. Seeking out physical exercise, support from others, and individual time for self may also help. Relationships are constantly growing and changing; sometimes people grow together and sometimes apart. Taking care of ourselves in healthy ways is imperative.

Relationships: New Beginnings and Endings

Although people are similar, they are also different. Each person is raised in a different family, with different views, holidays, cultures, socioeconomics, religion, values, and other life situations. Because of this, not all relationships last forever. One component of a relationship that often brings sadness and sorrow is endings. Sometimes in a relationship, one person may decide he or she is not ready for the relationship to end while the other one terminates the connection. This may cause pain and hurt feelings. There are times when one partner wants to end the relationship and move on, and the other partner does not want an ending to occur. This emotional pain may bring many feelings and thoughts, and an individual can become stuck in his or her emotions. The person may talk about the pain caused by lack of contact or information shared that the person did not want to know. This of course elicits many different emotions and at times confusion. Below is a fictional example of someone living in the past.

> Betsy previously dated Joe and remains emotional about thcir relationship. She is excited about her new relationship with her boyfriend Michael. When Michael and Betsy go to places, such as restaurants, the theater, or the park, Betsy has difficulty not talking about her previous boyfriend. She often shares activities that she and Joe enjoyed together. This situation has caused problems for both Michael and Betsy. She is not finished with her past relationship and continues to bring it into her present relationship. There is nothing wrong with missing Joe and remembering him fondly, however, Betsy is stuck in the past and not ready to move forward. She is missing both the present moments and the future moments with Michael. This continues to create a conflict in her new relationship.

*****Exercise*****

1. Create a list of past moments you feel stuck in, or that have previously caused conflict.

   _____

   _____

   _____

   _____

   _____

   _____

2. Please think about body awareness, in other words, where you feel these emotions in your body. Then write down the emotions experienced and where you feel them in the body.

   _____

   _____

   _____

   _____

   _____

   _____

*This exercise may bring feelings related to grief and loss.

- If sadness is the feeling brought forward, allow yourself to experience the emotion of sadness, tears, and memories, and then practice letting it go.

- If at any time it becomes overwhelming, give yourself a break to process the emotions and memories, and return to this activity later if you choose.

Being present-focused is an important component for each of us. Although the past and future are significant in our lives, it is important that we are not always looking back and wishing for something that was, but no longer is, in our lives. Evaluating and reflecting on how the present fits in your life is significant.

Another area difficult for people is denial or stuffing feelings. Often this involves not addressing the issue, which may resurface in life repeatedly if not addressed. Denying your emotions and not allowing yourself to grieve creates additional stresses. Sometimes, when people are struggling with hardship and do not want to feel the pain, they work to numb the pain and push it down deep inside. They may believe it will just disappear. However, we know that grief does not just go away. The process may be slowed, however, the emotions sometimes return more intensely and must be addressed for a healthy life. In grief and loss, emotions can be intense, overwhelming, and even physically painful. Because of this, sometimes people decide not to feel. However, deciding to put your feelings on hold for a long time, or ignoring them for years, will not help anyone move forward; usually these emotions will return and often more intensely.

For example, I worked with several individuals who lost their homes in the housing market crisis of 2008. It was devastating for them, as they had to make enormous changes in their lives. They worked on their grief in moving forward, but then did things that sabotaged their process. Two of the adults talked about going to their old house, sitting for hours outside in their car, and crying. Then they went to the home and thought about harassing the new owners. As you can imagine, this would create many additional problems and increase their grief process.

Another area of difficulty is experiencing a situation of death and loss. Grief and loss is a complex topic and a natural process. People often experience intense feelings, emotions, and physiological symptoms; they may decide not to grieve and create barriers to their emotions. Denying these thoughts and feelings, distracting yourself from them, and pushing them away often creates a barrier that makes grieving more difficult in the future.

There are times people may need to put their grief on hold, or on the shelf, for a short time. We know that acknowledging the grief and working through the stages of grief is necessary for the future. Choosing not to feel the emotions and blocking them does not work very long, and when the emotions resurface, they may be more intense.

Oftentimes, it is more helpful to reach out for counseling and work on the complex grief that you may be experiencing. If this would be helpful, please contact resources to assist in finding the best therapist for you.

There are times after a loss or death when people decide they do not want to be alone, and they become involved very quickly in new intimate relationships. Although this helps at times with loneliness and blocking the grief, it may create barriers and concerns with future roadblocks. Sometimes an individual will say he or she is just moving on, however, this may cause additional problems in the future. By ignoring the grief and "just moving on," the individual usually finds out that it does not always work. Instead, there may be a time when additional problems surface with more intensity, while this person continues to experience the stages of grief.

Example (not a real situation or person)

Imagine a husband whose spouse suddenly dies. He is devastated and tells himself, *I do not want to feel or grieve.* He is concerned with the intensity of the emotions and the significant pain, which are overwhelming. He chooses to ignore the grief of his wife's death and instead becomes involved in a new relationship, not allowing himself to experience the grief. This then leads to more problems in the new relationship, as he did not allow himself the opportunity to feel, grieve, love, and accept before he became involved with another person. Eventually the new couple separates due to the intensity and emotions of the loss. Later, this couple chooses to get support clinically through therapy; they work both individually and as a couple. The therapy includes both grief strategies and many tools. This relationship then takes a new direction, and in the end, they remain together, both healthy and happy.

When people live in their past for long periods, or if they rush forward into their futures, working to avoid the present, they often experience additional losses in their lives. They will miss the present moments, and this could be significant in their lives in moving forward.

Whether it is beauty, insight, a moment in time of happiness, sadness, or a sudden awareness, present moments have important places in our lives. Being in the present moment allows us experiences that often guide us in new directions or to new opportunities for the future.

CHAPTER 8

Goals: New Beginnings and Creating an A to Z Plan

Every great dream begins with a dreamer. Always remember,
you have within you the strength, the patience, and the
passion to reach for the stars, to change the world.
—Harriet Tubman

Setting Goals

What is a goal? A goal is something that we identify and create an action plan for. We then begin the task of working through the steps to accomplish the goal. The action plan is filled with the stepping-stones of a map, a journey, or a path; these help us accomplish what we want or need or help us change our behavior. Sometimes it is challenging to identify the goal, but goals are a part of our everyday lives.

They can be short-term, such as getting out of bed, getting dressed, attending school, interviewing for a new job, or being brave and talking to someone new. They can be long-term, such as planning a wedding, which would include identifying a date, planning a budget, creating a guest list, booking a venue, and determining the details of each step to accomplish the goal.

For some people, identifying the goal is easy and it flows; for others, it is difficult to think about the next step in moving forward. Goals help us to identify what is important to us, which could be almost anything.

The first area to begin with in goal setting is identification.

1.   What is the goal and why is important to you?
2.   What will the goal accomplish?
3.   Is it realistic and attainable?
4.   Is it short or long term?
5.   Who needs to be involved?
6.   What is the A to Z plan?
7.   What is the intention for the goal?

Please be aware that at times people may become overwhelmed with the goal process. Take a breath, go slowly, and know that slowing down, or taking baby steps is always possible in any situation.

When I was much younger, I believed in, and strived to accomplish, it "all." I was married, had two young children, worked two jobs, had pets, took academic classes, owned a home, owed bills, worked to eat a healthy diet, exercised, socialized with friends, honored my faith, taught religious school, and worked to have time for myself. That was a mouthful and I needed a breath just to finish the sentence.

I do not think this was realistic and it did not work; instead, it created more concerns in my life. Although I strived to accomplish all of this, what began to change in my life was my health and well-being. Exercise and healthy eating began to lag and I ate comfort food. I had no time for sunshine, no time for me, and no time for exercise. Because of the unrealistic expectation that I placed on myself, I began to suffer. I knew in my heart that my highest priority was my children, my family, and my work. In my head, my children were always number one and I was usually last on the list of everything. I began to realize that everything else began to suffer. The house appeared cluttered, there was no time for exercise, and we would eat easy to prepare food that was not always healthy. There was no time to socialize or do things for myself. My body was moving a mile a minute, my thoughts were racing, and I was doing great—or was I? This was not a realistic plan, and the person who suffered the most was me, along with my weight, my exercise, and my alone time; something had to give. I was unwilling to allow it to be my children or my career.

There are times people let themselves regress with their health, well-being, relationships, social time, and personal time. Accomplishing it all is not a realistic plan, but there are many factors to take into consideration.

This begins with acknowledging if a goal is realistic, then setting clear and specific objectives, evaluating the details of the goal, and knowing and understanding the reasons for the goal. In addition, one must identify an appropriate time commitment and have the flexibility to modify the goal. For example, a goal of losing twenty-five pounds in one week is neither realistic nor attainable unless accomplished in a very unhealthy manner.

Another area that may be difficult for people, is asking for help. Sometimes people may feel as if they are a burden, or that others believe they are not strong or smart enough. This may make them feel less valued or worthy. It is important to understand that asking for help is not a sign of weakness; instead, it shows strength and courage. If someone needs help, then asking for help is okay; however, if asking for help means having someone else do the job for you, then this is no longer a healthy alternative.

Steps in Working on Goals

As listed above, the beginning of the goal is identification. People identify, set, and accomplish goals every day—almost every minute. For example, if my patient is at a skilled nursing facility and the goal is to reduce depression and tears, then this goal is now recognized. The next step would be to identify if the goal is realistic and attainable. This must be determined first. If the patient is lying in bed twenty-four hours a day and the room is dark, one task could be for the patient to open up the blinds for twenty minutes a day and look out the window. This would be both realistic and possible, if the individual is committed to the goal.

With the goal identified and determined to be realistic, the next step in the plan would be to list the details and write down a step-by-step action plan. I call this the "A to Z Action Plan."

This A to Z Action Plan will pinpoint each specific step necessary to accomplish and succeed at the identified goal. However, remember to be flexible and allow for change in a necessary component of each step in the plan. Also, take your time; it does not have to become overwhelming and stressful. Allow each item to be evaluated, worked on, and accomplished before moving to the next step. Then check it off and give yourself a star, sticker, smiling face, or some other reward.

For instance, the patient has completed the goal three out of five days. However, on the fourth day, the patient is ill and slept throughout the day. In my assessment, this patient is still accomplishing the goal, but may have either had a setback or made a conscious decision to modify the goal. Therefore, creating balance is important to the overall goal. This patient needs to be commended for the steps he or she accomplished toward the goal.

The last task is intention. What is the intention and why do you want to accomplish this goal? I believe that intention is the defined purpose or attitude toward the goal. When you begin to define your goals and directions in life, you want to define your true intentions, write your action steps, find motivation, and pursue the steps toward that goal.

One of my goals is to give back to the community and help make a difference for others. I do this by providing some type of service, make a donation, or perform volunteer work, which helps to make the community a better place. This goal helps me in giving back to others and feeling an appreciation for my hard work and dedication. I volunteer monthly with a team to assist children who are in the foster care system. I also work several times a year at a camp for economically disadvantaged youth that gives them an opportunity to participate in a residential summer camp experience with many other volunteers. I encourage you to join me in volunteering. Identify a goal that you would like to achieve and that will help others. It could be assisting people, the environment, animals, or an agency. Giving back to others makes a difference in their lives and yours. In fact, often what begins as a way to give back becomes a gift itself.[23]

---

[23] Anna Beth Lane, "Research Shows That Volunteering Makes Us Happier," Community Health Network, accessed September 3, 2021, https://www.communitytechnetwork. org/blog/research-shows-that-volunteering-makes-us-happier/.

Many years ago, I worked as a school social worker at several Title 1 schools. Title 1 is a federal educational program serving low-income students throughout the nation[24]. These funds pay for additional educational services to help students achieve and succeed regardless of any disadvantages. At the time, I was at middle schools working with seventh and eighth grade students. After school, I facilitated a social action club and worked with these students on helping make a difference in the community. The students met weekly and decided they wanted to have a field trip and do something for others in the community. They agreed to make personalized cards for residents at nursing homes, collect socks for adults at shelters, and do something for children in Phoenix. The students were concerned that since they did not have money, they could not do anything. They said, "Mrs. Wall, we are poor students and we can't do anything." I decided it was time to teach a lesson on social action, about how anyone has the ability to do something for someone else. In fact, I believe it is our job to help repair the world through kindness, smiles, teaching, guidance, volunteering, and donations. The students discussed the goal they had and began to develop the A to Z action plan. They chose to volunteer their day at Thomas J. Pappas School, a school for at-risk, disadvantaged children experiencing homelessness in Arizona.

---

[24] Becky Spivey, "'What Is Title 1?' Handy Handout #386: What Is Title 1? Accessed," *"What Is Title 1?" Handy Handout #386: What Is Title 1? Accessed*, 0AD.

Eighteen of the middle school students and I went on this field trip, ready to make a difference in the lives of these children. I remember my students being amazed that many of the children at Pappas had more difficulties than they did. However, they connected to these elementary children, helped them with their school assignments and projects, laughed, and played with them all day.

On the bus ride back, many of my students were tearful as they processed the experience. Some of the discussion was about the children not having homes; some were living under bridges, in hotels, or in shelters, and some nights they had no dinner to eat. As my middle school students thought about their experiences, they smiled and laughed, and were happy they made a difference. They were clear that even though they felt as if they couldn't make a difference, they did more than they thought was possible. One of the students said, "Mrs. Wall, thank you for helping us make a little difference." I corrected them and stated, "You have given a little piece of yourself to someone else, and you have helped to repair the world, one baby step at a time. Be proud of your successes, and know that you made a difference for many today." We sang songs on the bus the rest of the way back and they felt pride in making a difference in someone else's life.

Two Goals and Intentions:

1. Write a list of two goals you would like to accomplish.

2. Write your intentions for the goals.

3. Write the A to Z Plan with all the details to accomplish these two goals.

4. Now, pat yourself on the back and say, "Good job me."

_____

_____

_____

_____

_____

_____

_____

_____

_____

_____

_____

_____

_____

_____

_____

Balance, Harmony, and Alignment: Where to Begin

To me, these words elicit a calm feeling, a sense of stability, and peacefulness. Thinking about balance, harmony, and alignment provides me with a sense of comfort in both mind and body. Visually, I begin to see the symbol of the yin and yang and it's balance. I think about balance in the body such as the right and left, two eyes, two arms, and two legs. Balance exists in our lives, in our bodies, and in our minds. How do we create a sense of balance and harmony? Being off balance can create great consequences for us, and sometimes we may even take a fall.

One day I was putting groceries away; my vision was blocked due to carrying too many items. I did not want to make another trip back to the car. I remember thinking, *I am almost there. This is heavy, and I need to balance. Please do not fall.* As I walked closer to the refrigerator, I felt a cord under my feet and lost my balance. At first I thought, *I can catch myself, I will not fall.* What I did not realize was there was a step and then a misstep. Suddenly, I was sailing in the air. I could feel myself no longer having any control, no longer being balanced. With a thud, I fell hard and hurt myself. I was off balance, out of alignment, and no longer feeling any sense of harmony.

How do we create balance in our world and a sense of harmony in our lives? The following story is true. I have received permission to share and I hope this story helps to make a difference in many lives.

Many years ago, I experienced great sadness when my sixteen year-old niece was a passenger in a horrific car accident, which nearly took her life. She spent six months in the hospital in a coma. Her injuries were extensive and included a broken neck, a severed limb, head trauma, and other medical concerns. When she awoke from her coma, so many things were different. She began to work on her long and extended recovery. She fought to relearn, modify, and create balance in her life. She needed to relearn how to eat, talk, walk, and do other things. She needed to find motivation, courage, strength, and support to recuperate.

One of the many challenges she experienced, and lives with today, was the severing of her arm. Coping with the loss of a limb brought grief and changes to her life. However, with her parents' support, the expertise of staff, and her commitment to change, she learned and modified her life in new ways. These immense changes in her life affected her balance. She learned to modify how she walked, she moved, ate, picked things up, and opened items. These were just a few of the many tasks that she needed to modify in her life. She lives her life with sensitivity, humor, kindness, and connection to others. It is a true miracle that she has modified her life with balance and harmony.

I believe that balance and harmony are areas of our lives we need to find and maintain. Having balance in our bodies, minds, and everyday activities is an important component of life. In fact, it is a critical component in our health and happiness.

My niece's life was very different from her life before the accident. She needed to identify and find her own internal strength, to muster up her motivation and determination, and to relearn most of life's tasks. In time, with her own internal strength, the love of her parents, family, and friends, and the support of medical staff, she found what worked for her.

Most people are gifted with balance in their bodies, having two eyes, two arms, two legs, and ten fingers, all of which assist in balancing the body. In her situation, she needed to adapt and modify her world to use one arm, one hand, and five fingers. She has done an amazing job finding what works best for her and strives to show others that working hard makes a difference.

Although this situation was devastating, life changing, and frustrating at times, it was also an amazing gift. She is here with all of us, helping to make a difference in this world. Because of a horrific accident that changed her life completely, she has increased her appreciation, strength, awareness, and sensitivity. She continues to make life meaningful by assisting others as a teacher and leader. Many people have no awareness of a challenge such as this. However, she uses her experience to teach the preciousness of life and the lesson that, with determination, hard work, and commitment, most things may be possible.

Balance and harmony—true gifts—we learn from her. She learns from us, and together we unite in both balance and harmony.

CHAPTER 9

Self-Talk: Positive Versus Negative with Tools for Change

The greatest glory in living lies not in never

falling, but in rising every time we fall.

—Nelson Mandela

Everyone has talk in his or her head. I describe it as self-talk, or speaking and processing to yourself, not aloud. It is hearing your own voice and giving yourself guidance and advice. I call this listening to your inner voice, which at times is positive but could be negative. Have you ever heard someone say, "Do you see the glass as half-full or half-empty?" Identifying whether your thoughts are more positive and optimistic or negative and pessimistic is important in a person's daily success.

In a previous chapter, there was a discussion of the number of thoughts a person experiences in his or her day. These thoughts are often constant in someone's mind. It is helpful if we work to keep the thoughts positive and supportive rather than negative. One way to do this is by redirecting the negative thought to a positive thought, writing down positive messages, saying positive words or messages aloud, and surrounding yourself with positive people. These are all strategies for redirection and may assist with positive thinking.

Example

You are getting ready to present a project at work. The team will be there, and your performance could lead to a large promotion and a wonderful raise. You begin to think about the details and then talk to yourself in your head. *How am I going to make this presentation the best possible presentation and get the promotion? What do I need to present?* Suddenly, thoughts take over and you begin self-talk: *I am ready. I know exactly how I will create this presentation. I am confident. I will speak loudly, and use humor at times.*

On the other hand, maybe your thoughts are negative: I *am not prepared. I know I should have spent more time organizing, practicing, and preparing.* These examples are of positive and negative self-talk or the messages you say to yourself. They are powerful and can begin to sway you in a direction. Each person has the power to redirect thoughts and use positive self-talk. The first step is being aware of your thoughts and if you are using positive or negative self-talk. The second step is redirecting these thoughts to positive self-talk and continuing to feed yourself these positive messages. The final step of success is moving from negative thinking to positive thinking.[25]

Examples of Messages

*   **Negative self-talk:** I am not good at cooking.

    Redirect to positive self-talk: I am working on improving my cooking skills and did a good job last night with the spaghetti and meat sauce.

*   **Negative self-talk:** I cannot do math and will never be good.

    Redirect to positive self-talk: I am getting better at math and have a tutor who helps me learn.

These examples represent strategies to redirect from negative self-talk to positive self-talk and they are realistic and genuine. Working on this tool can make a big difference in people's lives. Sometimes individuals have experienced others sending negative messages, words, statements, and put-downs. However, by using redirection and positive self-talk, a person can gain self-confidence and achieve a higher self-image.

---

[25] Mayo Clinic Staff, "Positive Thinking: Stop Negative Self-Talk to Reduce Stress," Mayo Clinic, posted February 3, 2022, https://www.mayoclinic.org/healthy-lifestyle/stress-management/in-depth/positive-thinking/art-20043950.

Change the Channel: Redirect the Thought

When I was growing up, there was no such thing as remote controls. If you wanted to see a different program on the television, you had to get up, go to the television, and change the channel. You did not sit down; you stood up by the television and waited until the commercial was over. You watched and if you did not like the program, you changed it again. People often laugh when I talk about this, especially people who have never had to stand up, watch commercials, or not use a remote control to change the channel. All kidding aside, think about this.

In negative thinking, we often have thoughts spinning in our minds repeatedly and it is often overwhelming. Therefore, one tool I teach is called Change the Channel. I describe it as making a noise with your tongue, like a click, then putting your hand to your head and changing the channel. This is funny, but true. It is something that people say is very helpful. My kids would often say to click your tongue, put your hand by your head, and imagine a dial that you change. "Now, change the channel."

One of the therapeutic treatment modalities often used by therapists is Cognitive Behavioral Therapy (CBT). This treatment modality is effective for a range of different problems. Cognitive behavioral therapy is an empirically supported approach to psychotherapy characterized by teaching individuals a set of coping skills. These skills are intended to modify maladaptive cognitive, behaviors and psychological responses that maintain and/or exacerbate psychopathology. The approach is present-focused and problem specific.[26] CBT is based on the idea that how we think (cognition), how we feel (emotion), and how we act (behavior) all interact together. Specifically, our thoughts determine our feelings and our behaviors.[27] CBT teaches many coping skills, which assists in problem-solving techniques, and helping to create positive changes. Below is another exercise to practice these skills.

---

[26] Kelly Drake, Courtney P. Keeton, and Golda S. Ginsburg, "Cognitive Behavioral Therapy (CBT)," Johns Hopkins Medicine, accessed November 9, 2022, https://www. hopkinsguides.com/hopkins/view/Johns_Hopkins_Psychiatry_Guide/787145/all/ Cognitive_Behavioral_Therapy__CBT_.

[27] Saul McLeod, "Cognitive Approach to Psychology," Simply Psychology, last updated 2020, https://www.simplypsychology.org/cognitive-updated 2019 therapy. html.

*****Exercise*****

Change the Channel: List five negative self-talk messages and redirect them to five positive self-talk messages that are realistic. Then practice this tool daily and watch your confidence grow.

1. _____

2. _____

3. _____

4. _____

5. _____

Boundaries and Self-Protection

Boundaries and self-protection are key areas that are helpful for you to understand and implement. When people think about boundaries, they may sometimes be confused. There are times people do not realize that what they say or do may affect others in negative ways. Often this is unintentional, but it may create conflict in people's relationships.

Example

A mom turns to her son and says, "Sometimes I worry about you, about what you are thinking and doing. I wonder if you are stupid or something. How many times have I told you not to do this?" These hurtful and negative words often create negative feelings. Most likely, the only words in this conversation that the son will remember will be "Are you stupid or something?" Is this really the message someone wants to relay?

It is possible to use boundaries as tools to protect yourself so you do not internalize these negative words, thoughts, or situations. They are not yours to own, so not allowing yourself to ingest the negativity and belief is imperative in your growth. I learned a version of the following technique from Lisa Williams at a conference many years ago. Lisa taught the tool by using light. I then expanded this technique by creating a different shield. I often use this tool for protection and teach it in my practice.

Tool: Lucite Box (used for negative words and energy from others)

A Lucite box is a box made of very thick plastic. It usually will not shatter or break, but may crack from within. This reminds me of safety glass that you may see on your car windshield. If a rock hits the window, it creates a star or a crack, but usually does not shatter the window.

Close your eyes, quiet your mind, and visualize placing a Lucite box two inches above your head. Then imagine it being moved down your sides and under your feet, protecting your entire body. This unique box is your protection shield and you are inside—safe, secure, and stable. It is just you in this protective shield and you may make it as big or as small as you wish. You can stand, sit, and dance in this imaginative protective shield. It reminds me of the invisibility cloak in the Harry Potter books. This shield will assist you with boundaries of protection, not allowing you to absorb negative energy, hurtful words, and negative thoughts. It is important to take time using your creative mind to imagine this box of protection, practice visualizing often, and work on boundaries.

*****Exercise*****

Close your eyes and imagine seeing a clear, strong, and supportive Lucite box. Now imagine placing it in a protective way for you. It is a shield and you are safely inside, ready for protection. Now open your eyes and believe you are protected. When someone makes negative statements about you, you are protected with your shield, and no longer need to absorb any negativity. It is not yours to take on and there is no reason you should absorb someone else's energy. The negative words will instead hit the protective box and bounce back, not allowing you to absorb any of the negative energy. *I am clear that everyone knows this, but if this negativity ever changes from verbal to physical, getting real protection is necessary, not using an invisible tool.*

Example (not a real person)

Someone says to John, "Why aren't you smarter? You never understand." John already has his Lucite box up and ready to go. He is protected, so when this person says these negative and hurtful things, they hit the invisible Lucite box and bounce off, never touching John. He uses his Lucite box and is protected from the other person's negative words and energy. Practicing this exercise often will help. Even if you think it is silly, it can and has been very successful. It allows you to stay safe and not absorb the negative energy or words of others.

Everything has energy; some energy is more positive and some more negative. Be aware of whose energy it is; if it is not yours, do not take it—give it back, and do not absorb the negativity.

At times, people can be very negative and it is not necessary for anyone else to absorb the negativity and take on someone else's energy. Taking time to establish your boundaries and protect yourself is important.

1. You do not deserve any negativity or someone else's energy.
2. You do not need to take this on; if it is not yours, give it back.
3. You are valued and worthy.
4. Use boundaries for protection to keep yourself safe.
5. Do not allow others' negativity to cause a problem for you. If it is not your energy to absorb, then let it go.

Example (not a real situation)

You are in a relationship for the second time with the same person. You are in love with this person and want to be together. However, this partner has ended the relationship before and now wants to rekindle. You have been thinking about this for several weeks and have decided that the relationship is worth working on one more time. However, this time you will create boundaries and protection, and make sure your partner hears your words and honors them. You state the following.

> I believe this relationship is worth working on, however, I will no longer allow myself to be treated negatively. If we return to this relationship one more time, and you decide the relationship is over again, then I will be done, and finished with this relationship permanently.
>
> Let me be clear: the relationship will be over and I will move forward without you.

This is an example of honoring yourself and being clear while protecting yourself with healthy boundaries.

*****Exercise*****

Example:

a) My goal is to eat a healthy diet.

b) I will not allow others to sabotage my eating or my exercise.

c) I will create my A to Z Plan.

d) Daily I will eat healthy meals. I will shop on Sundays, prepare food, and record what I am eating.

e) I will work out three to five times each week by walking or going to the gym for thirty to forty-five minutes.

 ❖ Identify five areas that you will work on to increase your healthy boundaries.

 ❖ Write down the specific steps.

 ❖ Specify the strategy you will use to protect yourself in healthy boundaries.

_____

_____

_____

_____

_____

_____

_____

Self-Image and Self-Awareness

When you think of *self-image*, what comes to mind? Close your eyes and see the word in your mind. What do you see? I see

_____

_____

_____

_____

Self-image is a personal view or image that we have of ourselves.[28] Many people have completed this exercise previously and reported that when they see the word *self-image*, they imagine themselves in a negative light. They might see themselves as short, overweight, unhealthy, having poor skin, not fitting in with a group, or have other negative thoughts.

Where does your view of self-image come from? Maybe it comes from your upbringing, the perception you have chosen, other people's perceptions that you have taken on, or experiences throughout life. These may include how you feel about yourself and the messages that you received from others.

There are times people are negative and critical of themselves. They may even live in constant, negative thinking, unwilling to believe their

---

[28] Cleveland Clinic, "Fostering a Positive Self-Image," Cleveland Clinic, accessed November 9, 2022, https://my.clevelandclinic.org/health/articles/12942-fostering-a-positive-self-image.

value. In addition, they may not realize they have a voice and the ability to speak up and advocate for themselves in a healthy manner. This also may bring up old patterns that keep someone stuck in a negative and unhappy place. There are ways to change this, but first it is important to allow yourself to redirect your thinking.

Tools: Affirmations and Mirror Work

Affirmations are positive statements that honor the self. I begin by introducing affirmations and then practice them. I teach the power of the words, the meaning behind sentences, and the intention set by the individual who creates and practices the affirmation. These are positive words and messages, which are spoken aloud with strength and meaning, and are, repeated multiple times each day. This provides the ability to really hear the words and understand the messages. Oftentimes individuals may not believe these positive statements, but in time and with practice, they will hopefully honor and believe these truthful messages.[29]

I met Louise Hay many years ago. She was an incredible author, speaker, and businessperson who helped make a difference in many peoples' lives. As stated at the beginning of the book, at fourteen years of

---

[29] Catherine Moore, "Positive Daily Affirmations: Is There Science Behind It?," Positive Psychology, accessed September 12, 2022, https://positivepsychology.com/daily-affirmations/.

age, I read one of her books. This set me on a path of change. I continue to have gratitude for her and her work, and encourage you to review her books and website (www.louisehay.com). These offer an opportunity to continue learning more about affirmations, the power of the mirror, and many other tools.

In my practice, I work with many tools, skills, and interventions. One tool I use is affirmations with mirror work. I begin by talking with the person about the changes he or she wants in life and together we evaluate if they are realistic. Then the person creates a sentence and reframes the statement in a simple and specific way. Affirmations are statements that allow people to redirect their thinking from negative to positive. After the affirmation is identified, written, and ready to be used, it is then combined with mirror work. I believe that mirror work is a very powerful tool to use. The eyes are intricate. Looking deep into the eyes becomes powerful and often encourages positive change and growth. Sometimes individuals may feel less than or that the affirmation will never be true. However, with consistency and follow through, the statements often become real and the individual's belief system begins to change.

*******Exercise*******

Examples of Affirmations

- "I am working on being the best me possible."
- "I will speak up for myself."
- "I am a good person and like who I am."

The second area we work on is identifying sentences used at home daily for follow up.

Below is another exercise for you to work on. Take a breath and know you are doing a great job.

1. **First week:** The individual identifies a statement.

   Example: "I am a good person. I am valued and worthy. I am beautiful inside and out." The individual identifies the statement, writes the statement on a notecard, and tapes it to the bathroom mirror. For the next week, the individual looks at the statement posted on the mirror and memorizes it.

2. **Second week:** The exercise continues.

   I ask the individual to say each of these affirmations ten times aloud, clearly and with conviction, while looking in the mirror into his or her eyes. The person repeats this activity twice a day.

If this activity brings tears to the person's eyes, I encourage him or her to move slowly and gently, as he or she gains strength inside. At times, I encourage the individual to focus on someone who believes in him or her. If there is no one, then please allow me, the author, to be the one who believes in him or her.

3. The individual continues to commit to working on this exercise twice a day, ten times in a row. The person looks into the mirror, deep into his or her eyes, and really sees who he or she is. Then the person continues to say aloud each sentence slowly and clearly ten times in a strong and meaningful voice.

Once again, mirror work is very powerful and will assist in this process over time. This exercise needs to be consistent, intentional, and practiced two times daily for thirty-one days. After the person has completed the affirmations for thirty-one days, he or she will often choose to move forward with the same tool but create another affirmation and continue his or her success.

Example: Mirror Work and Affirmations (not a real person)

Dazzle, a twenty-three year-old female, has experienced many traumas in her life. She reports a diagnosis of bipolar disorder and anxiety disorder. She attended counseling and after three months of working together, she begins mirror work and affirmations. She practices mirror work by looking into the mirror, deeply into her eyes, and sees the sparkles and brightness of her eyes.

She understands the uniqueness of the activity and that the eyes are the true soul, her true self.

When you look into someone's eyes, really look into someone's eyes, you begin to capture who he or she really is. As she practices the activity, she is encouraged to see the brightness, the light, and her true self. Initially, she was unable to look at herself in the mirror and experienced both tears, pain, and sadness. However, after several weeks, she has been able to see herself in the mirror, see her eyes, her soul, and her true self. She no longer has tears and becomes more comfortable in the activity. She is committed to working on this mirror work by saying the following affirmations ten times in the morning and ten times in the evening for thirty-one days.

First Affirmation: (state each affirmation ten times, twice a day)

- I am beautiful and kind. (Breathe.)

Second Affirmation

- I am a good listener and friend. (Breathe)

After thirty-one days of this activity, she realizes how successful she is and chooses the next affirmation. She then begins again with a new affirmation.

Third Affirmation (beginning after the others are completed)

- I am loveable and valuable to others and myself. (Breathe)

Beginning to identify our strengths and abilities and valuing them is a healthy outlook that should be important for all of us. There are times others have said untruths about us, and we may believe them and feel badly about ourselves. However, focusing on getting out of our heads and into our hearts often will assist in finding a better direction.

Tool: Journaling

Writing is a tool that can also be very healing. There are many writing activities, which include, but are not limited to, journal writing, free writing, prompt writing, and writing with meditation. Finding and purchasing a special notebook can make this writing activity more meaningful and easier because everything is located in one place. This is your special notebook and only for you.

However, sometimes people like to use an app on their phone, iPad, or computer. There are many ways to use this tool.

Here are three suggestions:

1. Write daily. Include highlights of the day, both positive and negative, and any insight experienced.

2. Create a topic page and write freely on one page each day.

3. Work on quieting your head, do a mediation, and then write about the experience.

4. Ask yourself a question and then write the answer that presents.

Example

Topic: Dreams. An individual takes a breath, closes his or her eyes, asks what dreams he or she has had, and then begins writing. The person should not think or focus on grammar, but just write. If the individual is working with a therapist, the journal may be helpful in counseling.

Connection to Self

This important topic oftentimes is disregarded. When speaking about connection to self, often people do not think about taking the time to listen to themselves, really quieting their minds, and listening to their hearts. Knowing people experience many thoughts per hour, it makes sense that quieting the mind can be challenging. Racing thoughts are also a concern at times. Taking time to sit quietly and be present in the moment is important.

Self-reflection is another area that people need time to work on. This requires being able to recognize who the person is and how the person feels about himself or herself, his or her body, and his or her life. At times, this may feel more like a struggle and the process of self-reflection continues. Focusing on the mind, body, spirit, and heart often provides the person with more information. He or she can then continue to learn and gain more knowledge about himself or herself.

I believe strongly that the mind, body, spirit, and heart integrate together, making an individual most connected to self and the direction of his or her future. It begins with quieting the mind and becoming aware of the heart and feelings. Quieting the mind, using diaphragmatic breathing to slow things down, and focusing on the breath helps with this process.

Take five to ten minutes and just relax using your diaphragmatic breathing. After about ten minutes, open your eyes. Think about the words *connection to self.* How would you describe your connection to yourself? What words go with you and your connection?

_____

_____

_____

_____

_____

_____

Example:

Work on listening to your intuition and your awareness of self. Pay attention to how you feel and what you know. Listen to the sounds; be aware of the surroundings: the crystal blue sky, the wispy white clouds, and the hummingbird that just hovered near you. Nature and our surroundings give us a lot of information.

Connection to self, who I am: "I am strong, courageous, kind, and loving."

*****Exercise*****

Zig Ziglar, an author and motivational speaker, wrote this: "What defines us is how well we rise after we fall." This is a unique statement. Think about this sentence: "What defines us is not how we fall, but how we rise after the fall." What do you think that means for you? Take a minute to write out a few sentences that fit for you.

_____

_____

_____

_____

_____

Each day brings a new beginning, and we have the opportunity to make the day bright and successful or frustrating and dark. Thinking about the sentence above can bring up emotions of success or failure. Often, we are so quick to quit or end the situation that we short-change ourselves.

Failure is a word that brings up many thoughts and emotions. When evaluating our response to this word, it is important to remember that if we continue to work on the situation, then failure never really occurred. I believe it is only when we quit, with no reason, that the situation may be considered a failure. However, sometimes it is necessary to end a situation. If you have looked at the situation, and it no longer is in your best interest or the healthiest choice, then maybe ending is the answer for you. If you make an informed decision to terminate a situation because it no longer serves you, maybe failure never really occurred.

Example:

A student signed up for a class in college. He registered, paid, and in the middle of the course realized he was not doing well in the class. He reached out to the professor, studied, worked with a tutor, and made a decision that taking the class in the summer might be a better choice for him. He began to create a plan. If he took the class during the summer, there would be more time, the class would be at a community college, the grade would transfer, and the cost would be less. He would have more time for the coursework and it would be his only class.

In this scenario, the student has truly evaluated the best decision for him. Although he will have to drop the class, it will not appear on his transcript. He will have an opportunity to retake the course, learn the material again, and receive a better grade. Initially, he felt as if he was a failure. However, after assessing the situation and working on his A to Z plan, his decision will allow him to rise above. This student honored who he was and made the best decision for himself. This process included evaluating the situation both logically and emotionally, and not quitting or failing, but instead rising from a fall and growing in a positive way.

Redirection of Thought

At times, people will speak about the constant thoughts that go on and on in their heads. Even when someone works to quiet his or her mind, there are thoughts that creep into the silence.

As discussed before, most people have between 2,500 and 3,500 thoughts an hour. They may speak about increased racing thoughts that may focus on specific topics or situations. These thoughts may become so overwhelming that they are difficult to slow down or stop. The thoughts can take over and cause anxiousness, racing heart, sweaty palms, or shallow or rapid breathing. This may bring on worry, increased anxiety, and panic. At times, these racing thoughts are negative and overwhelming; they may even be distorted thoughts that have become true beliefs. However, there may be no truth or validity to these thoughts.

Take a moment and think back to a time when someone said something about you that was unkind and untrue.

Example: "You are fat and will never be healthy."

Think about the difference between negative and positive thinking. If we work on redirecting the statement above to a believable, positive statement, it might look like this.

- I know that I am beautiful and working on my health and body; or

- I am big and beautiful and no one will tell me anything different.

Sometimes it is easy to believe what someone else tells us, however, that does not mean it is the truth, or that there is any validity to the person's statement.

Redirecting negative thoughts to positive ones is an important skill that each of us needs to work on and teach others. Two parts used in this skill are positive redirection and affirmations. Learning and implementing these skills has the ability to redirect the negative thoughts toward a more positive outlook.

I believe that in time, research will prove that chemical changes in the body and brain happen when we use these different strategies; already research is being conducted in this area. A positive outlook creates a new direction in people's lives. Beginning to use positive redirection and affirmations is the start. There are times when people are very hard on themselves and have unrealistic expectations. Perfection is not possible, but getting close means working to be the best person possible. There is nothing wrong with identifying characteristics or goals for the betterment of oneself, but degrading, belittling, or putting oneself down keeps a person stuck in the negativity and in an unhealthy lifestyle.

Working to be the best version of you is the beginning of change. It is also important to understand that not every day will feel good or be successful, but each day is a new beginning to make changes and redirect to a positive place.

Here is a reality check: there are times we are not positive, or we feel sad, down, annoyed, frustrated, angry, or just blah, and this a reality. Allowing ourselves to feel these things is important; however, sitting in the muck for too long will not be helpful or healthy. Each person must decide how long to sit in this negative place. We all must make this choice and decide when to move forward.

Below is your next challenge. I have faith in you. Now it is your turn. Do you have faith in yourself? Are you ready for a positive change?

*****Exercise*****

Next challenge: Write a list of five negative thoughts you have had in your life history.

Then redirect those five negative thoughts to five positive thoughts. Please write those new thoughts down below. If this exercise is difficult, take a breath, be still for a few moments, and think about someone who is positive and optimistic that you know and enjoy being with. How might that person guide you in positive redirection?

Negative Thoughts

1.

2.

3.

4.

5.

Now rewrite the negative thoughts as positive thoughts.

1.

2.

3.

4.

5.

Great job. You should be proud!

CHAPTER 10

Communication and Listening Skills

I'm a very strong believer in listening and learning from others.

—Ruth Bader Ginsburg

As I sat in the room and started the process of interviewing, I realized I needed to find other ways to communicate with the man. He was very intelligent, had been in the professional world in his career, but due to a stroke could no longer communicate verbally.

Communication is a critical component that we use in all areas of life. Whether communicating with an infant, an individual who is ill, a teacher, or a parent, we communicate with verbal expressions, non-verbal gestures, mixed messages, symbols, drawings, and other tools. Making sure that we are effective in our communication is another important component. When we think about communicating effectively, we want to be simple, clear, specific, concise, and appropriate.

Another area of communication is the approach used. Words have immense power and meaning. The voice is bigger than people think and sometimes, instead of talking in a normal voice, people may shout or whisper. In addition, the tone of voice may be soft, comforting, defensive, angry, calm, or supportive.

Non-verbal communication is using body language, facial expressions, posture, and eye contact to communicate. Dr. Albert Mehrabian, author of *Silent Messages: Implicit Communication of Emotions and Attitudes,* conducted several studies on non-verbal communication. He found that 7 percent of any message is conveyed through words, 38 percent through certain vocal elements, and 55 percent through non-verbal elements such as facial expressions, gestures, and posture.[30] This is important in communication because people share many messages through their body language and facial expressions. However, there are times people do not recognize non-verbal cues.

The exact origin of the saying "the eyes are the windows to the soul" is unknown. Some say it is from William Shakespeare while others identify it as an old proverb.[31] When I work with individuals on communication, we discuss the importance of eyes and eye contact. Looking at someone when communicating is a helpful tool, unless it

[30] Albert Mehrabian, *Silent Messages: Implicit Communication of Emotions and Attitudes* (Belmont, CA: Wadsworth Publishing, 1972), Chapter 3, page. 43

[31] "Origin of: Eyes are the window to the soul," Idiom Origins, accessed October 30, 2022, https://idiomorigins.org/origin/eyes-are-the-window-to-the-soul.

is not appropriate due to culture or authority. For many, looking at someone and having appropriate eye contact conveys a form of respect.

Oftentimes, people will report they feel heard and listened to, and that they mattered, when someone took the time to be present and look into their eyes in a supportive way. It indicated that the other person was looking at them, paying attention, and, of course, listening to their words. For example, in a group I led with participants, we practiced healthy and supportive eye contact. First we spoke about being present and looking at one another in a soft and supportive manner. People in the group practiced this skill and then discussed how it made them feel. Several of the participants stated that they felt seen, heard, acknowledged, and validated. The group continued to practice the skill and then the participants took it home to use in their lives.

Another exercise I use when teaching communication in-group is one I call Back to Back. A person picks a partner in the group he or she does not know well. They stand facing away from each other, back to back. One of the people tells a story, while the other person stands listening. Then the second person repeats the story, word for word if possible.

The second part of the exercise is when the partners continue to stand back to back, but stand twenty feet apart. One person tells another story and the partner repeats the story. This part of the exercise is often more difficult because of other people working on the same activity, the distance between the partners, and the struggle of not hearing or looking at one another.

The final part of the exercise is to remain back to back but in two different rooms while telling a new story. The partners begin to realize the complexities of communication, how distance is a challenge, and how not facing one another creates many barriers in communication.

The partners often become frustrated or laugh because of the challenges of the exercise and of real life communication.

Think about this scenario. You are speaking to your spouse. You shout, "Can you please bring me the vacuum?" However, your spouse is upstairs watching TV and did not hear what you said. Therefore, you do not get the vacuum. This reminds us of the Back-to-Back exercise.

The next exercise we work on together is a contest within the group. Each individual chooses a topic and has two minutes to communicate to the whole group. The rules are the following: no talking, no voice, words, sound, or any verbal communication. The person may only use non-verbal cues for the activity. Each person in the group has an opportunity to participate for two minutes using non-verbal messages. Someone in the group records what the individual communicated as the group continues to guess the non-verbal cues. After two minutes, another person begins the non-verbal contest. For example, someone goes to the front of the room and in two minutes, he has acted out, with no words, stop, go, high, low, short, big, and wink. He then receives his score. The next person does the same thing, but cannot use any of the previous words. Think about how often non-verbal communication occurs in our everyday lives. Crossed arms, eye rolls, waving hands, and so many other gestures enhance our communication.

Listening

Do you consider yourself a good listener? Are you really present and paying attention in conversations? Many people struggle with being good listeners. Effective listening is a skill that people often do not learn, practice, and implement in their daily lives. Being present, taking time to pay attention, and observing facial and body cues are components of engagement when listening.

There are times people do not pay attention, or only want to respond to the discussion. On the other hand, maybe they do not listen to the information presented and interrupt with their thoughts and words. Because of this, they often miss not only the conversation but also the present moment with the person with whom they are sharing this experience. Feeling heard, being present, and knowing that the person is taking an interest in what you say is necessary in healthy communication.

Can you remember a time you were telling a story and were interrupted by someone telling his or her thoughts, experiences, or feelings? Often in communication, people are quick to respond. They may only want to tell their stories. When it is another person's turn, instead of hearing what the person said or commenting on the details of his or her story, they transfer the story back to them. This may also happen in communication where there is a conflict. Someone becomes upset or defensive, and the other individual may stop listening and tune out the conversation.

One of my friends often says, "Everyone has an opinion from their head to their toes." It makes me laugh, but she is right. It often appears that everyone has an opinion and wants to express it; however, listening is the important key in this discussion of communication.

An article called "We're Worse at Listening Than We Realize" states that we spend approximately 45 percent of our communication time listening and 30 percent of our time talking. We often spend our time thinking about what we are going to say next or, worse, thinking about something else entirely.[32] When someone is truly listening in the present moment, engaged in the conversation, and understands, this person is usually able to restate the specifics of the conversation.

There are different types of listening skills, but two we will discuss are active listening and reflective listening. Active listening is when you are present, looking at the other person, and hearing the conversation.

---

[32] Clay Drinko, "We're Worse at Listening Than We Realize," Psychology Today, accessed November 3, 2022, https://www.psychologytoday.com/us/blog/play-your-way-sane/202108/were-worse-listening-we-realize.

Reflective listening is when you take time to hear the other person, are present, and then paraphrase back to them the information shared. You give your partner your complete attention, hear the words, and understand the conversation, while not advising, but listening.[33] It is not about agreeing with the person; it is about being present with the individual. Allowing the person to feel heard, validated, and supported, as someone listens to his or her perspective.

One day, I was spending time with a dear friend. She appeared to be upset and we went to lunch to talk. I was engaged in the conversation and looking her in the eyes, listening closely, and just being there. At the end of the conversation, with tears in her eyes, she said, "I want to let you know that rarely in my life have I felt heard and really listened to. You were looking at me, you seemed to hear me, and you did not interrupt me." I thought to myself, *This can be difficult for me at times and I work hard not to interrupt. I like to ask questions and really make sure I understand.* She said, "I want to thank you because I feel better and really listened to."

I explained to her that in conversations, I believe it is important to feel listened to and heard.

During our conversation, I did not disagree with her or tell her what to do. I listened, asked questions, and together we came up with ideas

---

[33] "What is Reflective Listening?" Popular Vedic Science, last updated May 22, 2022, https://popularvedicscience.com/ayurveda/general-health/what-is-reflective-listening/.

related to her concern. She stated she was appreciative and felt heard, that her words mattered, and that she had a voice.

Now I am certain that many people do this and work to be good listeners, so put your hand on your back and say, "Good job me."

CHAPTER 11

Thankfulness: Honoring Self, Now and Always

Acknowledging the good that you already have in
your life is the foundation for all abundance.

—Eckhart Tolle

Feeling gratitude, understanding gratitude, and showing gratitude
help us in our daily lives. A feeling of appreciation, thankfulness, and
gratitude is a task I work on daily. If you have gratitude, it seems as if
things are more positive in your life. In addition, I also teach this topic
in my practice. I assist people with understanding the importance of
being appreciative and thankful in daily life. Gratitude may be one of
the easiest and best-kept secrets to making wonderful changes in life,
especially if we focus on using it consistently.

In an article called "The Science of Awe," Summer Allen discusses
in detail the study, science, origin, and benefits of gratitude. Benefits

include better physical and psychological health, greater happiness and life satisfaction, less materialism, and more.[34]

Another exercise I use and teach is entitled Five a Day. Each person gets two special notebooks. One notebook is for all activities and tools and the other notebook is titled "My Gratitude Journal." This is the title at the top of the first page. I discuss gratitude and its importance on our daily lives, then each individual identifies a definition of gratitude and the importance of it in his or her life. Each day, the person records the date in his or her gratitude journal and writes the numbers one through five. Then the person identifies five things he or she is grateful for each day and which are different from any other day. If someone has difficulty writing, then he or she might find a specific time to do this aloud, or have someone else assist with writing.

Examples

- Taking a walk and being grateful for the beautiful sunset, sunrise, and stars in the sky.
- Gratitude for your child going to dinner with you, or spending time going to the park.

---

[34] Summer Allen, "The Science of Awe," Greater Good Science Center, accessed October 31, 2022, https://ggsc.berkeley.edu/images/uploads/GGSC-JTF_White_Paper-Awe_FINAL.pdf.

- Thankfulness for a beautiful song, story, or someone smiling at you or calling on the phone.

- Spending time with your beautiful dog, cat, or other pet.

Gratitude and thankfulness are everywhere. Identify it, acknowledge it, and feel appreciation and gratefulness for the many things in your life.

The time is now. What are you grateful for? Start your gratitude journal today.

- Get a new special notebook. At the top of the first page, write "My Gratitude Journal."

- Each day write the date and the numbers one to five. Identify the five things you are grateful for today. Then continue this activity tomorrow.

- At the end of each week, read aloud all the wonderful messages in your life.

Date: _____

1. I am grateful for the music I am listening to and dancing.
2. I am grateful for my dog spending time with me today.
3. I am grateful for the conversation I had with a new friend.
4. I am grateful for the Oreo cookie I ate that was delicious.
5. I am grateful for the wind and rain that watered my plants.

CHAPTER 12

Conclusion: Appreciation and Gratitude

Testimonials

Roxana

I began working with Suzi almost 4 years ago after starting medical school and realizing that my feelings of sadness, irritation, and agitation were more than just feelings of stress and burnout. She helped me realize how to work through my depression and anxiety by teaching me many strategies to use when feeling especially low or nervous. Together we worked on deep breathing, gratitude journaling, and writing. In addition, we would focus on how to change the mental channel in my head, which normally led me on a path of ruminating on negative thoughts, or a feeling of spiral[ling] out of control. Suzi also helped build my confidence and supported me in seeking out a psychiatrist for medications to help with my moods after a period of extreme depression. She really uses a whole-person approach and this has helped improve many aspects of my life in order to improve my mental health. She remains flexible and understanding with my busy schedule, and provides a perspective that I did not know I needed. After working with Suzi for the past few years, I can more quickly recognize unwanted negativity and manage my feelings more effectively.

Neal

I am an eight-year-old boy in Scottsdale, and I have been working with Ms. Suzi for almost two years. She has helped me be the best person that I could be. She helped me do well in school, and taught me ways to deal with difficult situations, and be nicer to my brother, and other kids. I had trouble controlling my body and I would get angry fast. She taught me belly breathing and techniques to help me feel safe. I still see her once a month to continue to work on being the best person that I can be. This last year in second grade, I ended the year with straight As and the award for most improved in the whole second-grade class. I found good friends who care about me with Ms. Suzi's help. I am very happy that my mom found Ms. Suzi to help me.

Don V.

I began my grief counseling several months after my wife of forty-six years passed away. At that point, my grief was extreme, almost a physical pain that lasted most of the day. It was difficult to think of anything else. The exercises and discussions in the sessions really began to make a difference for me. Getting my feelings expressed and adding new perspectives led to gradual changes in my feelings. Not that the grief vanished, but I did not have to obsess over it daily. I could begin to remember positives in my life with her and not just the painful things. One exercise that I found helpful was reviewing my life in five-year increments. It was very helpful as it provided me with a view of my life, both my good fortunes as well as my traumas. Another helpful exercise was to divide life into things you have control over and things you do not. This results in a variety of new perspectives for me. I also attended a few grief group sessions with other agencies, which I did not find helpful. The people in-group were not attending individual counseling and seemed stuck in their grief even after years of mourning. It was actually depressing to attend. After a year passed and having gone through the "firsts"—first Christmas, anniversary, birthday, etc.—I began to think of what is my next chapter. While always checking on the grief aspect, the focus of sessions shifted to my future. How do I fill my days, hobbies, volunteering, work, travel, etc.? In addition, I have a large family and there is usually some drama. It helps to have someone to discuss these things with especially since my wife is gone. Recently I have begun dating and have gained insights in sessions into dealing with other women after not dating for forty-eight years.

Male, forty-five years of age

March 2020 was when it all went downhill for me. COVID started to sweep across the United States and I was sent home to work from my house for fifteen days. Fifteen days long passed and after one month of being locked in my house, I began to notice I had a lot of anxiety when I did go shopping for the necessaries. I was not nervous about getting COVID; I was anxious about being in society again, around people. Normal human interactions were giving me anxiety. The original fifteen days turned into one year of working from home and when it was time to go back to work, I was a disaster.

I feared being away from my house for many hours; I could not be in meetings for an hour without feeling terrible anxiety. Everything I use[d] to do at work now filled me with stress and fear. I decided I wanted to seek help, because I could not and would not live my life like that.

I hopped on the computer and started to search for a therapist. I found Suzi and decided to try it. I am so thankful I did, because she was able to restore me to the previous version of me (and maybe even some improvements).

At the very beginning, Suzi gave me small tasks to do, such as mediation. I did it and that allowed me to see results right away. They were small results, but I was seeing progress and I knew I was on the right path. I continued with practicing what we would talk about during our sessions and I would apply it in my real-life situations. Soon I began to see a series of small victories that would give me confidence to continue. It took a lot of hard work, determination, and mental strength not to allow it to beat me. I am happy to say, after about one year of therapy with Suzi, I am about 90 percent back to my old self. I still have a little more to go and I will get there, I just need a little more time.

HTT

I thought I was fine, but my husband has told me that I have some emotional issues. I did not want to believe that it was true. One day, I suddenly realize that I got really, really angry for no reason. Then I decided to seek help. Suzi helped my husband, so I decided to schedule an appointment with her. I am glad I did and it has been a journey for me since.

I was born and raised in another country with a very different culture. However, the American culture fits my personality. My immediate family still lives overseas and I have many conflicts inside me. Sometimes, I feel lost. Some of my actions are appropriate in one culture, but are not in the other. I feel I am never good enough, and I keep trying to be perfect in both cultures, which causes me a lot of emotional distress. Sadly, before seeing Suzi, I did not want to admit my issues, and I did not know how to solve my problems. After seeing Suzi, she helps me recognize my obstacles. She gave me the tools to overcome my obstacles. Suzi made me realize that I do not need to always have the correct solution or be perfect. It is all about balance. I still have a long way to go, but at least now, I can understand why I had emotional distress and anger issues. Now I am able to see what my problems are and I continue to work on them.

Special Thank You

I want to thank the following people for granting permission and allowing me to share a little piece of them in the stories and the teachings they have provided.

A special thank you goes out to the following:

- Bruce and Matthew for assisting with the editing process;
- Matthew, Daniel, and Serena, for allowing a piece of your stories to be shared with others;

- Roxana, Neal, Don, Male Forty-Five, and HTT for granting permission to use their statements;

- The individuals who encouraged me to write this book and help others;

- My family and friends for making an ongoing difference in my life;

- You, the reader, for being a part of this journey; and

- Lastly, everyone who has played a role in my life. I thank you and wish you blessings.

Hearing, Seeing, Knowing, Feeling, and Being

This book has been a journey for me and I hope helpful for you. It began with planting seeds, nurturing them, watering them, and fertilizing them for growth. It moved to seeing a large tree with its trunk representing the structure and foundation. It has guided us through the branches moving in many directions, and the leaves budding, growing, and falling, which ended the winter season.

This book is a guide in honoring yourself—the true you—listening to your heart, and realizing that the head, mind, and brain are wonderful organs that assist us in finding who we are and honoring our hearts.

By using the strategies and tools in this book, you will grow stronger in your own hearing, seeing, knowing, feeling, and being. You will become skilled at listening to yourself, moving away from your doubt, and answering questions with confidence. Even if the choice you make is something you wish had been different, there is a reason you chose this branch on the tree. Find the way, honor your path, and know in the end that all is right for you. I thank you for allowing me to assist you with these skills, strategies, thoughts, and ideas. As you continue on your path and direction of life, may you evaluate the past and future while always living in the present moments and getting out of your head and into your heart. With gratitude and appreciation,

Suzi Usdane Wall, MSW, LCSW

A dedication to a unique and beautiful tree

BIBLIOGRAPHY

Allen, Summer. "The Science of Awe." Greater Good Science Center. Accessed October 31, 2022. https://ggsc.berkeley.edu/images/uploads/GGSC-JTF_White_Paper-Awe_FINAL.pdf.

Baikie, Karen A., and Wilhelm K. "Emotional and Physical Health Benefits of Expressive Writing." *Advances in Psychiatric Treatment*, 11, no. 5 (September 2005): 338–346. https://doi.org/10.1192/apt.11.5.338.

Brown, Brené. *The Power of Vulnerability: Teachings of Authenticity, Connection, and Courage.* Read by Brené Brown. Boulder, CO: Sounds True, 2012. Audiobook, 6 hr., 30 min.

Cherry, Kendra. "Biography of Psychologist John Bowlby." Verywell Mind. Last updated March 29, 2020. https://www.verywellmind.com/john-bowlby-biography-1907-1990-2795514.

———. "Erikson's Stages of Development." Verywell Mind. Accessed August 3, 2022. https://www.verywellmind.com/erik-eriksons-stages-of-psychosocial-development-2795740.

———. "Trust vs. Mistrust: Psychosocial Stage 1." Verywell Mind. Accessed March 7, 2021. https://www.verywellmind.com/trust-versus-mistrust-2795741.

Cholle, Francis."What Is Intuition, and How Do We Use It?" Psychology Today. Accessed October 30, 2022. https://www.psychologytoday.com/us/blog/the-intuitive-compass/201108/what-is-intuition-and-how-do-we-use-it.

Cleveland Clinic. "Diaphragmatic Breathing." Cleveland Clinic. Accessed October 30, 2022. https://my.clevelandclinic.org/health/articles/9445-diaphragmatic-breathing.

———. "Fostering a Positive Self-Image." Cleveland Clinic. Accessed November 9, 2022. https://my.clevelandclinic.org/health/articles/12942-fostering-a-positive-self-image.

Delagran, Louise. "What Is Spirituality?" University of Minnesota. Accessed October 30, 2022. https://www.takingcharge.csh.umn.edu/what-spirituality.

Drake, Kelly, Courtney P. Keeton, and Golda S. Ginsburg. "Cognitive Behavioral Therapy (CBT)." Johns Hopkins Medicine. Accessed November 9, 2022. https://www.hopkinsguides.com/hopkins/view/Johns_Hopkins_Psychiatry_Guide/787145/all/Cognitive_Behavioral_Therapy__CBT_.

Drinko, Clay. "We're Worse at Listening Than We Realize." Psychology Today. Accessed November 3, 2022. https://www.

psychologytoday.com/us/blog/play-your-way-sane/202108/
were-worse-listening-we-realize.

Fagan, Carolyn. "Top 25 Best Meditation Resources and Guided
Meditation Apps." Psycom. Accessed October 28, 2022. https://
www.psycom.net/mental-health-wellbeing/meditation-resources.

Johnson, Jon. "What to know about diaphragmatic breathing." Medical
News Today. Posted May 27, 2020. https://www.medicalnewstoday.
com/articles/diaphragmatic-breathing#summary.

Lane, Anna Beth. "Research Shows That Volunteering Makes Us
Happier," Community Health Network, accessed September 3, 2021,
https://www.communitytechnetwork.org/blog/research-shows-
that-volunteering-makes-us-happier/.

Mayo Clinic Staff. "Positive Thinking: Stop Negative Self-Talk to
Reduce Stress." Mayo Clinic. Posted February 3, 2022. https://
www.mayoclinic.org/healthy-lifestyle/stress-management/in-depth/
positive-thinking/art-20043950.

———. "Traumatic Brain Injury." Mayo Clinic. Posted February
4, 2021. https://www.mayoclinic.org/diseases-conditions/
traumatic-brain-injury/diagnosis-treatment/drc-20378561.

McLeod, Saul. "Cognitive Approach to Psychology." Simply Psychology.
Last updated 2020. https://www.simplypsychology.org/cognitive-
updated 2019 therapy.html.

Mehrabian, Albert. *Silent Messages: Implicit Communication of Emotions and Attitudes.* Belmont, CA: Wadsworth Publishing, 1972.

Merriam-Webster, s.v. "integration (*n.*)," accessed October 27, 2022, https://www.merriam-webster.com/dictionary/integration.

Mohan, Ronita. "Why Learning New Skills Is Good for Your Confidence." Thrive. Posted July 8, 2019. https://thriveglobal.com/stories/why-learning-new-skills-is-good-for-your-confidence/.

Moore, Catherine. "Positive Daily Affirmations: Is There Science Behind It?" Positive Psychology. Accessed September 12, 2022. https://positivepsychology.com/daily-affirmations/.

Newman, K.M. (2018) *Why is it so hard to be vulnerable?, Greater Good.* Available at: https://greatergood.berkeley.edu/article/item/why_is_it_so_hard_to_be_vulnerable.

"Origin of: Eyes are the window to the soul." Idiom Origins. Accessed October 30, 2022. https://idiomorigins.org/origin/eyes-are-the-window-to-the-soul.

Psychology Notes HQ. "The Two Hemispheres of Our Brain." The Psychology Notes HQ. Posted February 14, 2020. https://www.psychologynoteshq.com/brainhemispheres/.

Ratner, Paul. "New Controversial Theory: Past, Present, Future Exist Simultaneously." Big Think. Accessed September 30, 2021. https://bigthink.com/hard-science/a-controversial-theory-claims-present-past-and-future-exist-at-the-same-time/.

Sasson, Remez. "How Many Thoughts Does Your Mind Think in One Hour?" Success Consciousness. Accessed October 3, 2022. https://www.successconsciousness.com/blog/inner-peace/how-many-thoughts-does-your-mind-think-in-one-hour.

Spivey Becky. Title 1: Handy Handout #386: What is Title 1? Available at: https://www.handyhandouts.com/view Handout.aspx?hh_number =386

Thaguard, Paul. "What is Trust?" Psychology Today. Accessed October 30, 2022. https://www.psychologytoday.com/us/blog/hot-thought/201810/what-is-trust.

The American Heritage Dictionary of the English Language, 4th ed. (2000), s.v. "heart."

"What is Reflective Listening?" Popular Vedic Science. Last updated May 22, 2022. https://popularvedicscience.com/ayurveda/general-health/what-is-reflective-listening/.

University of Missouri-Columbia, "People Who Rely on Their Intuition Are, at Times, Less Likely to Cheat," Science Daily, posted November 24, 2015, https://www.sciencedaily.com/releases/2015/11/151124143502.htm.

Printed in the United States
by Baker & Taylor Publisher Services